FAITH, POWER AND PEACE

Faith, power and peace

THE 2015 SWARTHMORE LECTURE
DIANA FRANCIS

First published May 2015

Quaker Books, Friends House, 173 Euston Road, London NW1 2BJ

www.quaker.org.uk

© Diana Francis 2015

ISBN: 978 1 907123 76 4

eISBN: 978 1 907123 77 1

Book designed and typeset by Cox Design, Witney

Printed by RAP Spiderweb, Oldham

Cover image: Michael Menefee

While every effort has been made to contact copyright holders
of material reproduced in this book, the publisher would be
glad to rectify in future editions any errors or omissions.

Excerpt from 'Songs and Proverbs' is from *Border of a Dream* by
Antonio Machado (translated by Willis Barnstone). Used by kind
permission of Copper Canyon Press, Port Townsend, WA.

Excerpt on page 39 is from *The Gulag Archipelago 1918–1956: An
Experiment in Literary Investigation* by Alexandr I. Solzhenitsyn,
translated by Thomas P. Whitney and Harry Willets. In the UK
and Commonwealth (except Canada): published by The Harvill
Press and reproduced by permission of The Random House
Group Ltd. Worldwide excluding the UK and Commonwealth
(except Canada): © 1973 by Aleksandr I. Solzhenitsyn.
English language translation © 1973, 1974 by Harper & Row
Publishers, Inc. Courtesy of HarperCollins Publishers.

'First Dog on the Moon on the arms industry' cartoon by Andrew
Marlton. Copyright Guardian News & Media Ltd 2014.

Printed on FSC certified paper from sustainably managed forests.

THE SWARTHMORE LECTURE

The Swarthmore lectureship was established by the Woodbrooke Extension Committee at a meeting held 9 December 1907, the minute of the committee providing for an 'annual lecture on some subject relating to the message and work of the Society of Friends'.

The name Swarthmore was chosen in memory of the home of Margaret Fox, which was always open to the earnest seeker after Truth, and from which loving words of sympathy and substantial material help were sent to fellow workers.

The lectureship continues to be under the care of Woodbrooke Quaker Study Centre Trustees, and is a significant part of the education work undertaken at and from Woodbrooke. The lectureship has a twofold purpose: first, to interpret to the members of the Society of Friends their message and mission; and second, to bring before the public the spirit, aims and fundamental principles of Friends. The lecturers alone are responsible for any opinions expressed.

The lectureship provides both for the publication of a book and for the delivery of a lecture, the latter usually at the time of Britain Yearly Meeting of the Society of Friends. A lecture related to the present book was delivered at Yearly Meeting in London in the evening of 2 May 2015.

The Swarthmore Lecture Committee can be contacted via the Clerk, c/o Woodbrooke Quaker Study Centre, 1046 Bristol Road, Selly Oak, Birmingham B29 6LJ.

CONTENTS

PREFACE

My aim and hope in writing has been to support those who are already committed, heart and soul, to the rejection of war and pursuit of peace and at the same time to help those who struggle with this best known and central aspect of our corporate testimony.

During the many months of drafting and redrafting, I was acutely aware of global events that were unfolding, moment by moment. I could not write without reference to them, yet I was conscious that, by the time of the book's publication, they might take unexpected turns and the world scenario might look very different from what seemed likely then.

I can only trust that the reader will allow for that dilemma and any resulting dissonances, hoping that the underlying message will remain intact, and relevant to our faith and witness in a world that is in desperate need of both.

ACKNOWLEDGEMENTS

I have been supported by many Friends, friends and family members, mostly through their encouragement and their tolerance of my distractedness and preoccupation.

In particular and more directly I have been helped by the trust and feedback of the Swarthmore Lecture Committee and the unfailing accompaniment of my two appointed supporting Friends, Beth Allen and Philip Gross, whose counsel came in very different and complementary forms, so that I was constantly both affirmed and challenged.

In addition, I am deeply grateful to my friend and colleague of many years, Celia McKeon, who gave me close personal, professional and editorial support and an additional perspective that together were invaluable to me, and to Jan Arriens, who was there at the end of the phone when I needed encouragement and feedback.

Finally, Louisa Wright has been the most supportive and flexible publishing Friend I could ever have hoped for.

The ultimate weakness of violence is that it is a descending spiral begetting the very thing it seeks to destroy. Instead of diminishing evil, it multiplies it. Through violence you may murder the liar, but you cannot murder the lie, nor establish the truth. Through violence you may murder the hater, but you do not murder hate. In fact, violence merely increases hate. Returning violence for violence multiplies violence, adding deeper darkness to a night already devoid of stars. Darkness cannot drive out darkness; only light can do that. Hate cannot drive out hate; only love can do that.

MARTIN LUTHER KING, JR.

INTRODUCTION

Where I come from and what I want to do

I come from a family in which radical opposition to war was taken for granted. Both of my parents were conscientious objectors, my father to military conscription and my mother to recruitment as a munitions worker. They were Christians who saw the rejection of war as essential to their faith, for the same reasons that Friends do. It was from my parents that I inherited this belief and I was active in the peace movement from the age of fifteen – several years before I first encountered Friends. I came to Quakers thinking that here at last was a spiritual home in which I would no longer have to argue my case with fellow worshippers.

I was disappointed to find that this was not altogether true, yet I am glad, for a great many reasons, that I stayed. The Society of Friends is my home. And in the fifty years that have followed my first meeting for worship, my own beliefs in relation to war and peace have been only strengthened by the testing they have had in peace campaigning, by my work with local peacemakers in different parts of the world and by the spirit of love that I encounter in others, which sustains me.

In this short book I want to share with you my understanding of our calling, in the current state of un-peace that needs to be addressed; some reasons why I believe a resounding 'no' to war is not only a necessary concomitant of our faith but an urgent global need; and an alternative vision for the future, with some ideas on Britain Yearly Meeting's actual and potential role in giving life to that vision. I will be giving a good deal of attention to the doubts that I think hold us back as a Society, discussing war and violence at length and arguing that violence only perpetuates violence and that therefore it is essential for humanity to opt for another model of power.

Our peace testimony

Our peace testimony, as expressed by Friends through the centuries, is perhaps our most distinctive witness: the aspect of our testifying for

3

which we are most widely known and which sets us apart from many other faith bodies, giving us our status as a 'historic peace church', together with the Church of the Brethren and the Mennonites.[1] We have been given that label not because we try to have peace in our hearts and want to keep war to a minimum but, first and foremost, because we have taken a stand against all war, rather than following the 'just war' tradition, believing that this institution of organised, large-scale violence is, in any circumstances and for whatever reason, contrary to our faith.

Of course the rejection of war is only one side of our testimony to peace – arguably just the beginning. Friends also try to live in ways and engage in action that will help to prevent violent conflict and build a peace that is worthy of the name. Yet, as Ben Pink Dandelion said in his 2014 Swarthmore Lecture, the principled rejection of war was the starting point for Friends. Testifying against war came first in what we now call our peace testimony (Dandelion, 2014). In my experience, it is the hardest part to uphold (everyone is 'for peace'), and still the one that distinguishes us from most other people – people of faith and those of none. At the same time, I shall argue that unless the whole system of war is dismantled and faith in it dissolved, we shall never have the chance to build the peace we dream of. In any case, these two halves – 'no' to war and 'yes' to peace – need each other, both for their practical impact for good in the world and for the spirit from which they spring.

To this day, across our widely varied global Quaker family, this aspect of our faith remains a unifying factor: something of which we can be proud and which also presents us with a challenge. It goes to the very heart and basis of our faith: our experience of the spirit of love in worship and community, which affirms the teaching of 'one Christ Jesus' and leads us to the conviction that all human beings are, in Isaac Penington's words, 'unique, precious, a child of God'; to put it nontheistically, all incorporate the sacred and are born to love and be loved.

It is out of this experience and conviction that we testify to the world, saying with Friends in their declaration to Charles II, 'All bloody principles and practices we do utterly deny, with all outward wars, and strife, and fightings with outward weapons, for any end, or under any pretence whatsoever' (*Quaker faith & practice* 24.04), and this because, as George Fox put it, we 'live in the virtue [meaning 'strength'] of that life and power that [takes] away the occasion of all wars' (*Quaker faith & practice* 24.01).

Faith goes beyond having answers or arguments. Ours is a profound and instinctive conviction that arises from inner experience of a loving spirit that transcends our own lives and upholds commitment. It is our guide for living in the world, a yardstick so clear and an aspiration so deeply held that it can lead us through dark and difficult places and inspire creative and loving responses in seemingly impossible situations.

Yet it is very hard to square our faith with some aspects of human life and behaviour and the dilemmas which they present, and although it holds firm at the centre of Britain Yearly Meeting, many of us in our local meetings struggle to make that kind of faith commitment in relation to the peace testimony.

The problem for these Friends is not with the 'letting our lives speak' aspect of it, whether that means seeking inner peace and smoothing the troubled waters of their own lives, or supporting or taking part in constructive peace work in situations of violent conflict. It is the unequivocal 'no' to war that sticks in their throats. Their own honest doubts make that impossible and they call into question the rightness of a blanket rejection of war. At the same time, those who were drawn to the Society by the peace testimony and consider it to be central can feel that they are regarded as dogmatic and insensitive when they talk about this aspect of their faith.

I realise that people cannot be argued into faith and do not feel that it is the task of some Friends to supply all the answers for others, even if they could. It is for us all to recognise that this aspect of our faith is integral to who and what we are together, and to support each other as a faith community, in this as in all aspects of our common testimony to the spirit of love. This is simply my contribution to that ongoing process: a chance to explain why I believe we can and must keep faith and unite behind the whole of our testimony, setting ourselves a radical agenda for the coming years.

My aim is to help lift the doubts that hold us back, so that we can contribute wholeheartedly, from a common faith and vision, to the making of a better future, and to show that our hope is grounded in experience of a radically different, transformative kind of power.

To this end I will spend a good deal of time on the problem of violence and war. I will start with a short discussion of the terminology and concepts of conflict and violence, then set out the manifold expressions of violence and their impact that has made the time in which we are living a time of crisis. I will point to the alternative scenario that would become possible if there were a profound shift away from the power of violence towards a different kind of power: one that is already at work in ways that need to be recognised and uplifted.

I will then discuss at some length the obstacles to letting go of belief in violence as a means of doing good, examining the concept of necessary violence through the prism of Just War theory. I will then look carefully at different scenarios of violence that represent the toughest challenges to our faith and seem to some of us to support the concept of 'the lesser evil'.

I will end this first section with a discussion of the roles of nature and nurture in defining who we are, and the choices that are open to us, so paving the way for the next section, on power for peace. The final section, 'Agenda for transformation', looks to the future.

CHAPTER I

Violence and war

Conflict and violence

Although 'violence' is often referred to as 'conflict', the two words are not synonymous and it would help if they were not used interchangeably. Conflict is uncomfortable, but in itself it is neither good nor bad. When handled respectfully and constructively it can be the necessary route to addressing wrongs, reaching new understanding and improving relationships. Conflict avoidance often takes people into deeper conflict or chronically impairs relationships and collective functioning. It takes courage and care to deal with conflict in positive ways, but the capacity to do it can be developed.

Violence, on the other hand, is by definition that which violates or harms. When we recognise it we should reject and expose it and, when we have the power to do so, help to prevent or end it. In a brilliant and influential article, Johan Galtung suggested that violence takes the form not only of actions or behaviour but of structures or systems – social, political and economic – that subject people to injustice and indignity, and cultural beliefs, attitudes and norms that 'make direct and structural violence look, even feel, right – or at least not wrong' (1990, p. 291). He defines violence comprehensively, as 'avoidable insults to [meaning 'assaults on'] basic human needs, and more generally to life' (p. 292). (That 'more generally to life' is important to us.)

While my main focus in this book is on the direct physical violence that finds its apogee in war, all forms of violence run counter to our beliefs and to the spirit of love to which Quakers have testified down the centuries. That is why we work to displace them with ways of thinking and acting (embodied in different aspects of our testimonies) that uphold the dignity of others and honour their lives and needs: ways that can lead to 'positive peace'.[2]

---

2 Galtung explains the concept of 'positive peace' in an unpublished work 'Theories of Peace: A Synthetic Approach to Peace Thinking', in which he explores over 35 conceptualisations of peace. See http://www.transcend.org/files/Galtung_Book_unpub_Theories_of_Peace_-_A_Synthetic_Approach_to_Peace_Thinking_1967.pdf, especially p. 17 [accessed 29 December 2014]. See also Galtung (1964, 2005).

Violent dynamics in a time of crisis

As the third millennium gets under way, humanity is confronted by multiple threats that are liable to compound each other. For many around the world those threats have already turned into catastrophes. It is not beyond human capacity to prevent further deterioration and to cope far better with what cannot now be avoided, but adjusting to the impact of damage already done will be a huge challenge, both morally and technically. This state of affairs has been brought about by reckless greed and uncaring arrogance, backed by violent behaviour and exploitative systems of all kinds.

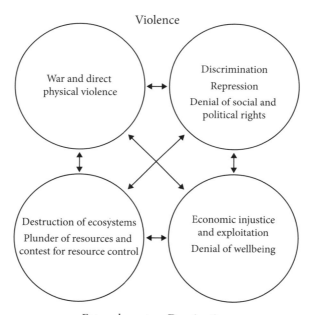

Eat-or-be-eaten: Domination

In the above diagram, I have represented four key aspects of this violence and the impact that each has on all the others. The word 'domination' at the bottom of the diagram encapsulates the approach to life and relationships that is expressed in all the forms of violence represented in the circles (an alternative approach based on interdependence and cooperation is shown in the diagram on p. 16).

The desire to dominate stems from an 'eat-or-be-eaten' view of life. It makes individual or collective self-interest the focus of all endeavour and regards the power to dictate terms to others as the means of serving that self-interest. It leads to exploitation of people and planet, and legitimises and uses direct physical violence as an instrument of power.

The violence of war and the negation of human rights and democracy

Wars are made up of acts of inhumanity which in any other context would be regarded as the worst kinds of human rights violations. They may involve acts of great courage and self-sacrifice, but there can be no doubt that this is a system that requires people to commit acts of extreme violence against fellow human beings: acts which, without the rubric of 'war', would automatically be regarded as utterly barbarous. Saying 'no' to acts and systems of inhumanity – torture, slavery, the death penalty, for instance – is not negative but a necessary and positive first step in upholding human dignity.

Down the ages, decisions to go to war have been taken by people situated at the top of power hierarchies. Once upon a time those people who took the spoils of war also put themselves in the front line (and sometimes, like King Harold, paid the price). However, most of the suffering was always borne by poor families, whose able-bodied men were pressed to fight, leaving the women to care for the children and old people, while the men were killing and being killed. Civilians were liable to be raped, slaughtered or burned alive at home, or driven from their land and forced to take their chance in strange places.

Somehow the suffering of individual human (and other) beings in war tends to be lost in the big picture of carnage, but war's true story is one of human suffering of unbearable intensity, on a catastrophic scale, among combatants and noncombatants alike; of a process in which 'victory' is gained by a combination of luck and killing power, not by moral superiority. That victory is liable to be hollow. To quote one saying from the Balkan wars, 'To the victor go the spoils and the spoils are a heap of ashes.'

The impoverishment that wars have always caused comes in many forms, beyond those associated with their immediate, direct impact. In terms of human values, wars both reflect and promote the idea that some people's lives and wellbeing (those of the poor and the enemy) are of no account. In the past, wars consumed the wealth of monarchs and chiefs and, through them, what was left of their peoples' small resources, requiring special taxes to pay for their prosecution.

The destruction caused by wars to crops and buildings created the need for costly restitution, and natural resources, like trees, were plundered for military purposes (such as the building of the ships of the British navy). And all this was liable to be repeated, so that the ostensible gains of one side were liable to be reversed by the other a few generations later. Meanwhile the lives of the poor remained as wretched as ever.

Has the picture changed? Not only are horrific numbers still killed by 'small arms' and machetes, but technology has played a greater and greater part in warfare, to the point where a single nuclear bomb can kill several million people (not to mention other living things). Even without 'weapons of mass destruction', the scale of killing per war has risen to a level that must once have been unimaginable.

Killing and injuring at a distance through the use of high explosives, in place of face-to-face fighting on the ground, reduces the loss of life on the side of the user but results in terrible 'collateral damage' in local populations. Sending drones from far away (supposedly so smart that they reduce the number of those killed unintentionally) is all too attractive. While it is easy and safe for the user, it does in fact cause many civilian casualties and indeed is done to terrorise local populations as well as to assassinate the individuals targeted.

Economic violence and marginalisation

The 'eat-or-be eaten', dominatory approach to life is manifest not only in direct violence but also in the current state of vast, global and local economic inequality, produced by an economic system that makes the rich richer while failing to address poverty. As a result, a shameful proportion of the world's population endures varying degrees of material deprivation, excluded from the wellbeing that comes from knowing that there will be food and shelter, education and medical support for oneself and one's family.

According to the Stockholm International Peace Research Institute (SIPRI), world military expenditure in 2012 (the latest date given) totalled US$ 1,753 billion. Perhaps it is worth repeating here the famous quotation from the speech made by President Eisenhower in 1953, known by the title 'The Chance for Peace':

> Every gun that is made, every warship launched, every rocket fired signifies, in the final sense, a theft from those who hunger and are not fed, those who are cold and are not clothed. This world in arms is not spending money alone. It is spending the sweat of its laborers, the genius of its scientists, the hopes of its children. This is not a way of life at all in any true sense. Under the clouds of war, it is humanity hanging on a cross of iron.[3]

The extreme inequality of relationships Eisenhower describes, and the mechanisms that perpetuate it, constitute a systematic assault on basic human needs that Galtung would term 'structural violence'. It is often combined with discriminatory policies and social practices that cause marginalisation and exclusion of all kinds, which cause grinding poverty and migration that in turn often create conflict and violence between settled populations and desperate others who are seeking a place to settle. These conflicts intensify and are exacerbated by perceptions of religious, tribal or ethnic identity.

Global inequalities of wealth often result from the imperialism of the past and the neo-imperialism of the present. The 'haves' are those who have inherited the spoils of the past and who dictate terms to the have-nots. This syndrome entangles us all in its unseen and complex dynamics, whether we are included in or excluded from material wealth, in our own society's terms or globally. It has a gender dimension, in that women are often economically dependent

---

3 Eisenhower made this speech following the death of Stalin, only shortly after he himself took office as President of the United States of America. The full text is available at http://en.wikisource.org/wiki/The_Chance_for_Peace [accessed 29 December 2014].

(though highly economically productive) and in many societies are still excluded from inheritance and ownership, being effectively 'owned' themselves.

In this way and others, social and economic exclusion are interrelated. Discrimination in one sphere creates injustice in others – further 'avoidable insults' to basic human needs, both psychological and physical. The security that comes from social and economic inclusion should be seen as a human right, something we owe each other, just like political freedom and participation. Furthermore, hunger and deprivation, social isolation or humiliation, imprisonment and torture are all, I would argue, violations of that part of the human spirit that 'knows' what we all owe to each other. In his influential Swarthmore Lecture of 1981, *True Justice*, Adam Curle pointed to the 'hidden conflict' of oppression as a major cause of the open conflict of organised violence, equating the true justice of his title with peace; and oppressive relationships are in themselves maintained by overt and systematic violence. Both greed and grievance are drivers of war (Berdal and Malone, 2000).

Violence to the ecosystem

The concept of human rights is well established. That of animal rights has joined it more recently. Recognition that our whole ecosystem has needs that must be honoured has been slow to develop, and has been even slower in being translated into the radically different behaviour that is required for the sake of all species and indeed for the future of life on earth. Pam Lunn's Swarthmore Lecture of 2011, and Friends' response to it, marked the fact that, for Britain Yearly Meeting, protection of our planet had finally arrived as an integral aspect of our collective testimonies. The war economy and wars themselves are environmentally devastating.

Within this framework of understanding, just as action that is an assault on the basic needs of another human being is violence, so is action that constitutes an assault on the basic needs of earth's whole ecosystem – including those of its human population. The impact of the eco-crisis on basic human needs and rights has already been catastrophic in the poor world, where countless lives and livelihoods have been destroyed by floods and drought, and chronic water shortages cause misery and conflict.

Resource shortages that increase deprivation not only cause misery but also stand in the way of the reduction in population growth that would help preserve the web of life on our planet, by denying people the levels of education and security that would enable them to opt for smaller families. Both the human population and its levels of consumption need to come down and the rich need to change their lifestyles radically.

Violent conflicts over resources, fuelled by the desperation of people immediately affected by threats to their subsistence, cause yet more misery and poverty, through the killing or maiming of labourers and livestock, and destruction of crops. Even more seriously, in ecological terms, the greed of powerful nations for future resource control drives wars that cause human suffering and violate human rights on a grand scale. They consume vast resources and destroy and pollute yet more, increasing poverty and ruining the infrastructure needed to address it.

In summary, these different forms of violence and suffering are the fruits of an approach to life that both relies on and generates direct physical violence in one form or another. War, and the culture and systems of militarism from which wars arise, are its most direct, acute and iconic expression, enforcing and driving the rest. In another witty slogan from the Balkan wars, 'If war is the answer, it must be a very stupid question.'

A different vision

For Friends, the experience of universal, transcendent love suggests a radically different vision: one which expresses our commitment to truth, simplicity, equality and peace with all people and with our planet; and a vision which can be glimpsed, perhaps, through the frame of the alternative model in the diagram on p. 16.

This second diagram represents a dynamic process of positive peace – the state of affairs that love requires – involving a radical shift from a dominatory to a cooperative approach to life, in the spirit of interdependence and mutual caring. It points to a radically different kind of reality: one for which many of us are already working, in one way or another, and towards which our central work in the world is orientated.

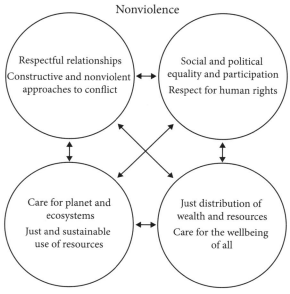

Nonviolence

Respectful relationships
Constructive and nonviolent
approaches to conflict

Social and political
equality and participation
Respect for human rights

Care for planet and
ecosystems
Just and sustainable
use of resources

Just distribution of
wealth and resources
Care for the wellbeing
of all

Interdependence – cooperation

Diagrams are no more than ways of giving visual shape to thoughts on some aspect of reality. In categorising and re-presenting, they must simplify its true complexity. In this case I have separated two very different approaches to life that in reality are intermingled and coexist. For instance, a particular community or society may be relatively supportive and peaceful internally but prone to great violence externally. (If we live in the UK, we need not look far for examples.) An economic system may produce some things from which a society benefits at the same time as having effects that are detrimental to the common good. The motivations of individuals are often (perhaps usually) a mixture of self-interest and altruism. And sometimes there is apparent competition between different needs, or the needs of different people, even after much creative thinking – in which case, with the best will in the world, difficult judgements will have to be made. Is it not possible, then, that those difficult judgements might involve, in some circumstances, countenancing the possibility of going to war?

Observation and reason tell me that endless pursuit of violent solutions to violence is disastrous for human beings and the planetary system of which they are a part. Faith tells me that human beings are capable of finding better ways of addressing their dilemmas; that organised, direct and deliberate violence, designed to inflict grievous harm on others, each one unique and precious, cannot be a solution to other forms of violence. To see it instead as a necessary option (and therefore institution) is to me a counsel of despair, rendering our faith empty and consigning the world to a very ugly future. Yet still I cannot simply dismiss the inability of some Friends to rule it out and will turn now to Just War theory as the long-established and still current framework for exploring the moral case for recourse to war in certain circumstances. I will also address the broader argument that war can at times be a necessary, because lesser, evil.

Just War theory

The early followers of Jesus understood that discipleship called them to follow him in rejecting the worldly power or rulers and armies, friends and enemies, and to embrace the power of powerlessness, vulnerability and love, not responding to violence of any kind with counter-violence but overcoming evil with good. For the first three hundred years of the Church's life, Christians, as a matter of faith, rejected war and military service.

With the conversion to Christianity of the Roman Emperor Constantine, the gap between Church and State closed, and this had a great impact on the mainstream approach to living the faith. In the new Christianity, as embodied in the Church as it became, Jesus's model of power based on freedom and love was displaced by the power model of an empire built by military expansion and domination.

This big leap away from early Christian teaching clearly left a residue of unease over the apparent moral contradiction, and the idea and principles of a Just War, which came first from Greek and

Roman philosophers like Plato and Cicero, were used by Christian theologians like Augustine and Thomas Aquinas as a basis for constructing a moral framework that could ease away that tension. The outcome of that process of accommodation has been that the Church, in many guises, has blessed the wars of states, and that indeed many wars have been fought in the name of Christianity.

Just War principles are related to lawful authority for war, to just causes and conditions for going to war, and to just conduct in waging it. One major condition that must be weighed before entry into war is the likelihood of winning it, since the good that it is estimated that the war will do must be in proportion with the violence used and the suffering that it is likely to cause. If the war is lost (and victory can never be predicted with certainty), that supposed good will be lost too.

In Just War theory, the only just cause or purpose for going to war is to redress the injury of a wrong that has been committed and, even then, war is justified only as a last resort. The ultimate goal of a war must be to establish peace, or to bring about a better state of affairs.

Finally, the strategy and weapons used in the war must make it possible for those waging it to discriminate between combatants and civilians and to obey certain rules in regard to the combatants themselves when these pose no immediate threat to life on one's own side.

Whereas Just War theory was originally intended to limit the waging and conduct of wars, making them less likely and curbing excesses in the ways in which they were fought, it is hard to regard it as effective, even in its own terms. It seems rather to have had the effect of giving credence to the idea that war can be a justifiable means of conducting human affairs. Both sides in wars will always argue that their cause is just and make a case for its conduct, and so the carnage has continued.

The dignity and supposed 'divine right' of monarchs, and subsequently of states and their governments, were deeply embedded in the cultures of countries launching wars, as were the status and authority of village chiefs or clan heads in differently structured societies. This kind of unconditional loyalty to groups of ethnic, political or religious belonging, as units to fight for and defend, remains all too prevalent (though recent years have seen greater public questioning at times, in the UK at least).

There has always been solidarity between the major political parties in the UK on what is euphemistically called 'national defence' policy, in terms of wars to be waged and weapons acquired, including nuclear weapons. The idea that a vote should be expected before wars are joined is a very recent one (perhaps representing a turning point whose importance we have not yet fully recognised). And, although lip service is paid to the United Nations, its backing is regarded as desirable rather than vital.

'The national interest' and 'national security' often provide the rubric for the justification of war, in place of any 'just cause' stemming from some specific injury inflicted on the people living under the 'legitimate authority' in question, although 'regime change' (argued to be necessary for the sake of 'the people' whose country is under attack) comes in sometimes as a secondary justification or as cover for the real 'national interest' reason, such as access to oil reserves.

In the case of the war launched against Iraq in 2003, the initial pretext for the war was that country's alleged nuclear weapons programme, which was cited as a threat to the security of other countries (unlike, presumably, the nuclear weapons of states that already had them). Although the move to war was supported by some on account of past atrocities against the Kurds and of other human rights violations perpetrated by Saddam Hussein's forces, regime change was not at that point the war's official objective, but it became the means of justifying it when the nuclear weapons allegations were proved to have been false. In fact, Iraq had been subjected to Western interference and instrumentalisation since World War I, and it seems clear that regional hegemony and control over the country's vast oil resources were the real motivation.

In this case (paralleled in many ways by the latest long-lasting war in Afghanistan), not only were the alleged 'causes' suspect, but the impact of the war on the Iraqi population, far from meeting the Just War criterion of establishing peace, has been devastating. Theirs had been a country in which, despite terrible human rights violations in particular areas, most people coexisted without fear of day-to-day violence or sectarian conflict. Human needs such as economic sufficiency, health care, education and infrastructure were relatively well met and the rights of women far exceeded those of most other women in the region.

After the 2003 Iraq war, the Iraqi people, of whatever identity, already affected by the sanctions that preceded the war and having lost more than a million of their number during its conduct, found themselves living in a country that was environmentally devastated and whose oil wealth went elsewhere, while basic services had been ruined. Life for ordinary people was not only hard but frightening, on account of sectarian violence, and the situation of women and their rights infinitely worse than they had been under Saddam Hussein.

More recently, the marginalisation of Sunnis, encouraged by the West, has issued in a terrible backlash that has greatly intensified the violence. The wider impact of that war is inseparable now from the general turbulence in North Africa and the Middle East, in particular the disastrous war in Syria. The answer of those who launched the 'shock and awe' bombardment of Iraq has (in 2014) been to launch new air strikes. Heaven knows what will have happened by the time this book is published.

Not only are the motivations and outcomes of these and many other wars at odds with Just War principles, but the very logic of war – even war in the Just War tradition – militates against the ethical constraints that should shape its conduct, in that it makes the determination to win a war integral to the justification of that war. From the establishment of this principle it is only a very small step to add ' – whatever it takes'. That is also why, even where the 'laws of war' have discouraged the rape, torture and deliberate slaughter of civilians, the principle of avoiding civilian casualties has been blurred by the notion of 'collateral damage' or unintended consequences, despite the fact that those consequences are known to be inevitable – for instance, when cities are bombed.

It seems that the lives of 'the other side' are of little account when compared with the lives of 'our soldiers'. Of course that fits with the goal of winning. Indeed, 'enemy' casualties, whether military or not (in either case human beings who matter), are usually not counted by the warring parties. I remember only too vividly the television images from the first Iraq war, of the bodies of long columns of Iraqi conscripts being dug into the sand after they were deliberately bombed as they fled back across the desert. Soldiers, too, are human beings, with complex lives, relationships and feelings, whether their reason for fighting is patriotism, religious ideology, coercion or a simple need to feed themselves or their families. The principle of the sanctity of human life cannot exclude them.

The war in Afghanistan was the first to come under the rubric of the 'war on terror': a new justification for war fighting (and other human rights abuses, such as assassinations by drone strikes, or torture and detention with no recourse to law). The term was coined in the United States in the wake of the attack on 'the Twin Towers' and the Pentagon. Under this banner, a state considering itself to have been injured by an act of terrorism committed on its territory claimed the right to avenge that act by taking whatever military action it saw as relevant. In this case that meant in the first instance launching a war against another country that was held responsible because it had allowed the presence of a terrorist organisation, Al-Qaeda, within its territory.

This war was launched without any serious pause for thought or space for negotiation: a hasty and a wholly disproportionate act of vengeance that has resulted in countless deaths of Afghans and a tragic number of US, British and other service men and women to add to the original toll of the September 11 atrocity. It did not vanquish Al-Qaeda, which was falsely alleged to be at work in Iraq before the Iraq war was launched, though it did indeed arrive there subsequently (and has now been displaced by other terrorist groups). The continuing discourse of 'the war on terror' is used to justify violent attacks on countries under suspicion and so to kill not only those described as terrorists (creating new martyrs) but also many civilians – only widening the divide between 'the West' and the people it attacks.

As for the 'likelihood of winning' criterion for a Just War, even very powerful states lose wars, particularly when the motivation of those on the other side is powerfully related to place, identity and control over their own affairs. The USA lost its war in Vietnam, and Afghanistan has resisted attempts at domination by a variety of powers. From what I have seen in my lifetime, the only thing that can be predicted about wars is the terrible misery and destruction that they cause.

The dead cannot speak, but should be remembered – not turned into mere numbers – along with survivors whose lives have been devastated. They can be all too soon forgotten, taken out of the moral scales, as has happened in the West in relation to the local people in Afghanistan, for instance, where improvements in girls' education in some parts of the country are often cited as justification for the war (along with the supposed reduction in 'terror').

I am suggesting that war, by its very nature, cannot be just, and that the very concept of Just War is part of the problem, in implying that it can. The same can be said for the secular, streamlined justification, which is based on three false assumptions of mythical status: that the 'causes' or purposes for which leaders go to war are indeed altruistic; that all alternatives are exhausted (that everything else really has been tried first); and that wars are indeed effective in achieving the good goals claimed for them (Francis, 2004). In practice these simpler but similar conditions are never applied.

Yet I am aware that the examples I have cited are relatively 'easy' ones with which to support my case. Even if we can agree that many wars are waged without just cause or good outcome, surely there remain cases where you cannot simply hang on to the idea of nonviolent love in the face of actions that are clearly wrong? Where there are indeed just and urgent causes, not only self-serving pretexts? Times when something must be done and when war, on whatever scale, is the lesser evil – better than just standing by?

I need now to focus on the hard core of cases that really challenge us. I will give some examples of such situations and examine the case for war's justification and its actual or likely level of success. Later, under 'Power for peace', I will look at nonviolent options for responding in different circumstances.

Moral crunch points

World War II
While the point or pointlessness of the World War I and its carnage

have been widely debated, the justness of World War II remains much harder to challenge. Hitler's rise to power can reasonably be seen as having been, at least in part, an outcome of World War I, in particular the punitive terms, for Germany, of the treaty that ended it. However, his military-expansionist agenda and programme of invasion clearly contravened international law and the rights of other peoples. Surely there was no choice but to answer fire with fire? And what about the Holocaust?

The first thing I must say here is that going to war against Hitler's Germany did not prevent the Holocaust and involved other gross atrocities, by the Allies as well as others: for instance, the fire-bombing of Hamburg, Dresden and Tokyo. The war resulted in a global conflagration in which victory was by no means certain and an unimaginable total of around sixty million human beings died. During its course the first atomic weapons were developed and 'tested' on two Japanese cities – atrocities on a grand scale – and the ground was laid for the Cold War and the nuclear arms race. I cannot understand why this vast and far-reaching catastrophe is so generally seen as self-evidently preferable to the likely outcome of any alternative, even if it were conceded that the only alternative available was utter surrender.

Could anything not involving a global conflagration have 'stopped Hitler'? It depends where you start, of course. Quite possibly his rise could have been prevented. He did not spring from nowhere. Had Germany not been humiliated and impoverished by the Treaty of Versailles at the end of World War I, a different sort of leadership might have developed there; and if the story had been different earlier on and dysfunctional European power relations had been addressed more constructively than by the terrible carnage of that 'Great War', things could have been altogether different.

As things were, however, given Hitler's growing popularity, building a global peace and solidarity movement across Europe could have supported internal resistance, and if that movement had led to a preventative equivalent of the post-World War II Marshall Plan, to rebuild Germany's economy right then, those steps could perhaps have prevented his continuing rise.

Even when his march of territorial expansion had begun, civil resistance within all the countries he occupied, had it been well prepared and organised, could have made his control of occupied countries extremely difficult. Even without such preparation, there was some resistance in the form of public acts of non-cooperation: for instance, by teachers in Norway when they refused to teach the Nazi curriculum, and by Dutch and French citizens when they hid Jewish people in their homes.

Such ad hoc and relatively small-scale examples of what can be done are not to be dismissed. Rather, we need to consider how much more could be achieved if civil resistance were undertaken by populations willing to defend their rights and freedoms and protect each other nonviolently. Much has been written on the subject of social or civilian-based defence by scholar-activists such as Brian Martin and Gene Sharp (see bibliography). They emphasise the importance of preparation, and Martin in particular has shown how a nation well prepared for this kind of resistance could make a very unattractive proposition for a would-be invader.

However we see these past events, since what was done was done, we are left with hypotheses. In the present, we can only think about alternatives for the future and act to ensure that we develop them.

Liberation wars

For several decades, 'liberation wars' were the ones to agonise about, if you really cared. As a young campaigner I was frequently challenged with the right of oppressed people to fight for their liberty.

Then and now my reply is that I cannot make moral decisions on behalf of other people, and that I fully understand why in some circumstances people decide to fight against their oppressors.

However, I have seen that liberation wars (for instance in Guatemala, Mozambique and, most recently, Colombia) cause great suffering to those who need to be liberated. The people get caught between the violence of the government and the violence of the revolutionaries; they are prevented from going about their daily life and are liable to be murdered for not submitting to threats and complying with the demands of one side or the other. The rebels may at last be crushed; and even if they prevail, what follows may fall far short of the dream. Often, after years of fighting, a 'mutually hurting stalemate' is reached and some sort of settlement is at last negotiated (sometimes by new, younger leaders who are more realistic than their elders and want a different future), or there may be military victory on one side or the other. Lasting stability and genuine peace are another matter. The toll of such wars is heavy; the dead remain present by their absence in the lives of the bereaved and their memory is passed on. The scars of violent conflict are deep and lasting. Nonviolent resistance has contributed at least as much as liberation wars to the ending of tyranny, and offers a principled alternative to the brutalisation and suffering of war.

Humanitarian wars

While 'liberation wars' are waged by those whose liberation is at issue, 'humanitarian wars' are waged on behalf of others, though on their territory. The Kosovo war, which was claimed by those who launched it to have humanitarian concerns as its motivation, became a new emblem of the 'need' for 'decisive military action' to right wrongs, and the notion of 'humanitarian intervention' was established as a new and altruistic incarnation of the Just War.

The myth that this war was both just and effective played an important role in rallying support for the Afghan and Iraq wars, when their original pretexts had been exposed or rejected and the fact that they had both far exceeded all expectations in terms of duration and casualties called for further justification. I will therefore examine in some detail the way in which that myth was constructed in the media and by government.

The crisis in Kosovo built up over decades. (It was called Kosova, with an 'a', by the majority of the population, who were ethnic Albanians, but over time 'Kosovo' has become the usual spelling in English.) During that time, under the leadership of Ibrahim Rugova, there was a determined campaign of nonviolent civil resistance to the removal of Kosovo's autonomy by Slobodan Milosevic and ongoing discrimination against Kosovar Albanians (Clark, 2000). However, when solidarity from elsewhere was needed and nonmilitary influence could have been brought to bear by countries wishing to support a just outcome, nothing was done and the Dayton Agreement confirmed Milosevic in power. As human rights abuses grew worse, armed resistance began, with the formation of the Kosova Liberation Army (KLA), and this in turn triggered concerted attacks on Albanians.

Alarmed by these developments, the Organisation for Security and Cooperation in Europe (OSCE), with the permission of the Serb government, sent a team of human rights monitors to Kosovo. The proposed number was 2,000, but in the event fewer than 1,300 were sent, and those ill-prepared for their task. Even so, the presence of these observers made a remarkable difference and, although there were still atrocities, these were far fewer in number. The response could have been to build their number quickly, adding experienced or well-trained personnel and providing additional training on the spot, and intensifying dialogue with Serbia, with the assistance of Russia.

Instead, the monitors were abruptly withdrawn, deadlines were set and, in the Rambouillet talks, the self-appointed 'international community' suddenly shifted its position, placing the idea of a constitutional separation on the table for the first time and proposing to send foreign troops into Serbia: demands that they knew Milosevic would consider impossible, given public opinion among Serbs at large. When he refused to sign, without any United Nations debate, it was announced that NATO 'had no choice' but to launch an attack.

As various military experts had warned, this did not halt the violence against Albanians in Kosovo. Instead, it was massively increased and the terrible exodus began, along with bombing in other parts of Serbia. Civilians of all ethnicities were killed. The infrastructure of Kosovo and the rest of Serbia was severely damaged; chemical pollution and the radiation from depleted uranium in warheads poisoned the region; the land was littered with deadly cluster bombs; and all hope of inter-ethnic coexistence in Kosovo was propelled far into the future.

The hatred engendered by the violence of the Serb militias and NATO's action was such that the space for inter-ethnic tolerance had been virtually eradicated. The Albanian population, seeing their aspirations for separation as having been vindicated, were no longer open to continuing within the same framework as Serbia, but demanded full statehood. Ethnic minorities and tolerant Albanians were intimidated and murdered. Serbs remained in Kosovo only under the protection of international forces, and Roma people were singled out and killed or forced to flee. (For a more detailed account of the Kosovo crisis, see Francis, 2001.)

Almost two decades later, Kosovo has been declared an independent state by Western powers, but its status is still a matter of international dispute. Russia continues to resent the West's arbitrary arrogation of powers and uses the creation of Kosovo's 'independent' statehood as a justification for its own behaviour in relation to South Ossetia and Ukraine. The participation of former KLA personnel, including known war criminals, in the highly sectarian governments in Kosovo has militated against good governance and human rights there. Tensions continue between ethnic Serbs in the north and the majority ethnic Albanians, and at the time of writing almost 5,000 NATO troops remain in the country to prevent the eruption of violence. A US military base so huge that two hills were flattened and a valley raised to accommodate it was constructed and remains in place, extending the global presence of the US military into a further strategic location.

Yet the impression left by the massive media coverage of this war (a coverage which, as usually happens, did not continue once the war 'ended') is based on the image of fleeing thousands which, once seen, was referred to as the cause of the invasion, rather than its immediate outcome. Most people are unaware of the true sequence of inaction and action by foreign powers. They do not realise that, after a decade-long absence of international solidarity with the Albanian population's little-publicised resistance, a promising effort at civilian protection was made or that it was accompanied by apparently serious diplomatic efforts, in which Russia was assisting and which had only just begun – in other words that, far from 'alternatives' having been exhausted, they were abruptly cut short in favour of a military onslaught.

Most people are also unaware that, quite apart from the war's immediate toll in destruction and displacement, its longer term effect has been to consolidate both local enmity and international divisions. And thus it has been used to bolster the reputation of military intervention as a humanitarian act.

It is hard to isolate this catastrophic episode from other events in the region, but solidarity at a much earlier stage for the nonviolent resistance undertaken by Serb Albanians, more support for cooperation between nonviolent activists across the region, and a principled and constructive role played by other states might have brought a far more positive outcome in what was Yugoslavia.

'Responsibility to protect'

The concept of a 'responsibility to protect' now constitutes a more or less established international norm, which builds on the notion of military humanitarian intervention. It was formulated, on the basis of pre-existing international law, in retrospective response to the massacres in Rwanda (1994) and Srebrenica (1995). The first principle of 'R2P', as it is often called, is that states have a responsibility to protect their own populations from wholesale atrocities and crimes, whether those crimes are categorised as ethnic 'cleansing', war crimes, crimes against humanity or genocide. The second is that 'the international community' (presumably, in this case, nations or forces working under the auspices of the United Nations) has the responsibility to support any state in meeting that primary obligation.

The third principle is that if the state responsible for preventing the criminal behaviour taking place within its jurisdiction shows no will or capacity to protect its citizens, and if peaceful measures at supporting it in doing so have failed, the international community has the responsibility to intervene through coercive measures such as economic sanctions. Military intervention is to be used only as a last resort, if noncoercive measures and nonmilitary coercion have failed, and authority to order it lies solely with the United Nations.

The belief that human beings have a responsibility for one another's wellbeing is one that Friends share, and I suspect that most Friends will be unfazed by the idea that national sovereignty should be overruled in certain circumstances. It is also likely that most will accept all the elements of R2P up to and including the point of nonmilitary coercion.

The concept of a responsibility to protect seems important,

altruistic and ambitious. Applying these ideas with any seriousness or consistency would presuppose a major shift from nationalism to internationalism and a global focus on the prevention of violence, with the provision of very substantial resources to back that policy. It would mean a transfer of decision making and resources from the big military powers to reformed, democratic international institutions and an end to spurious wars of protection. Radical and necessary changes indeed.

However, provision for 'last-resort' military intervention remains a problem, both in itself and because ultimate faith is still placed in military solutions – which is precisely what makes it unlikely that the necessary resources and commitment will be found for all the other steps to be implemented. The pressure for speedy action, together with belief in the efficacy of lethal power, would make it unlikely that other options – particularly supportive ones – would really be given a chance.

Furthermore, at the point of last resort, when prevention of violence is no longer an option because the violence has already begun, it is not clear that third-party violence can be effective in halting it, let alone in making peace. Military 'peacekeeping' cannot work where there is no peace to keep.

Where peacekeeping armies have been present with the intention of preventing outbreaks of violence in a tense situation and have not acted or had the desired effect in the face of atrocities, it would seem to have been, at least in large measure, because they have not known how to do so. This was the case with the Dutch peacekeepers who were present when the Srebrenica massacre took place and with the Belgian general who pulled his troops out of Rwanda as the genocide began. Peacekeeping efforts in Darfur had little effect on the determined violence of Sudanese forces and local militias. UN peacekeepers in the Democratic Republic of Congo (DRC), sent into an already hellish situation, have been unable to end the violence there and in many instances have become part of it. When those who are carrying out atrocities are literally mixed in with those they are butchering, as in Rwanda, or embedded in the population (as is the case with 'Islamic State' in some of the communities in which it operates), it is impossible simply to kill these without killing those, even if that would put an end to the dynamics of violence – which it cannot.

It is all too easy to expect a system that has been invested with mythical powers to perform miracles, but the real people who are given the responsibility of operating within that system may simply be defeated by the challenge of making peace happen by violence and in the midst of violence, rather than becoming part of war fighting. Presumably the reason why Britain put troops into Sierra Leone when it did and not sooner was, in part at least, because the violence had reduced to a level when peacekeeping was possible and the mission could play a positive role – with the help of local community activists – in stabilising the situation, so that the mending of a broken society could begin.

In Iraq and Afghanistan, years after the violence of invasion, with a huge occupying military presence, the violence from within has not been controlled. It remains an unquenchable fire. Yet the myth of violence's power for good remains alive, as evidenced in the case that was made for the bombardment of Libya, where it was suggested that a short phase of well-targeted bombing would end the violence and make way for peace – which of course it did not.

That bombardment not only caused terrible destruction in the country, and the slaughter of both soldiers and civilians, it also derailed efforts by nonaligned nations to broker peace talks. Those responsible for it remained silent when the former President, Muammar Gaddafi, was lynched, despite the fact that almost every European leader had physically embraced him the year before. In Libya now there is a situation of grim chaos, with local militias presiding in different parts of the ruined country, and the whole region is in a ferment of violence. The rest of the world seems powerless to do anything, for all its firepower, since the capacity of violence is to destroy, not to build or mend, planting deep the seeds of enmity for future generations.

The good news is that even in such extreme circumstances a glimmer of light remains. It is kept alive by local people who see the senselessness of what has been done and are determined to find ways of saving and regrowing ways of respectful coexistence. They meet and talk, sometimes seeking moral support and help from outside facilitators and trainers, as they identify the most fruitful ways of working. They are the hope for the future.

'Something must be done!'

The exclamation that 'something must be done!' is a sign of compassion, evidence of instinctive human caring and feelings of mutual responsibility. But that cannot be allowed to blind us to the fact that we may not be able to do anything that will help at a particular moment and that it is better to do nothing than to make things worse. To borrow Gandhi's words, 'I object to violence because when it appears to do good, the good is only temporary; the evil it does is permanent.'

Within the academic field of conflict studies, it is recognised that at the point of all-out war, any constructive intervention is more or less impossible. 'Conflict prevention' (i.e. the prevention of violence) is the obvious option. That means not only 'early warning' that things are going wrong, but early remedial action in response to those warnings – requiring levels of caring, will and provision that do not yet exist. Without that, often the best that can be done is to watch out for any opportunities to de-escalate and end the violence – find any pockets in the heat where a more benign and constructive kind of energy can be brought in. Once the will is there, a ceasefire can be brokered and the slow process of reaching a lasting resolution of the conflict and recovery from the violence can begin.

Human beings are not omnipotent and our responsibility cannot exceed our power. People with a commitment to working for the general good find this hard to accept, but sometimes – in a particular moment and place – people and governments are indeed powerless to help and it is better to accept that helplessness than to act destructively and make things worse. At the same time, there is a great deal of unalloyed good that humanity fails to do because such a vast proportion of our collective resources goes into the failed 'security' of militarism. Thus a whole world of responsibility to protect our fellows goes unaddressed while some of us wrestle with the particular single issue of protecting them against sudden outbreaks of gross violence.

Protection from starvation, or thirst, or death by waterborne infections and other preventable diseases is something that really could be provided, if the will were there and the resources made available. We somehow tolerate the knowledge of endemic human rights violations and the toll of preventable suffering from famine and floods, about which far more constructive action could be taken.

The Ebola outbreak that has been raging for months, as I write, has spread as it has because of the level of chronic and devastating poverty in the countries affected. Our government is reluctant to see lives risked to bring aid to refugees, where a much greater level of humanitarian assistance could transform acute suffering, or to welcome immigrants escaping from conflict zones or from persecution or desperate poverty.

Unpredicted atrocities assume such a focal position in our thinking because they are so sudden and dramatic, and more directly attributable to particular groups or entities than the cruelty of neglect (the violence of 'avoidable insults to basic human needs'). They are also the most avidly reported cause of suffering. Particularly when graphically presented to us, they confront us so powerfully with a sense of moral challenge that we simply fail to consider related decisions sufficiently clearly. The idea that violence can be kept in tight control all around the world by the instant application of more powerful violence is not only unrealistic but nightmarish.

'If all you have is a hammer, everything looks like a nail', and as long as the hammer of violence is the main tool we choose to invest in, we shall always be seeing nails in situations that are actually made of soft, diffuse or complex things that call for very different treatment. War is not designed for protection, and to use violence to control violence – although in some instances it may smother one source of it for a time – will ensure that it remains alive; and even the smouldering embers of violence can burn for a very long time.

It has been put to me that the idea of deterrence offers the possibility of preventing evil without having to do evil. This argument, I would suggest, has several serious defects. The first is that creating, maintaining and endlessly 'modernising' this kind of capacity consumes necessarily great resources that could otherwise be used to do good.

The second is that in order for a deterrent to be taken seriously the policy related to it must envisage its use in certain circumstances and therefore – where nuclear weapons are concerned – the commission of acts amounting to genocide.

The third is that belief in deterrence drives the arms race, both vertically – in terms of ever more deadly and expensive capacities – and horizontally – in terms of proliferation to countries wanting to join the club of those able to exercise such threats. Thus the danger to all continues to grow.

The fourth is the resentment that is liable to grow in those thus threatened. And the fifth is the moral and intellectual damage that such policies do in giving credence to the idea that might is right, perpetuating the myth that preparedness to commit great cruelty, by means available only to rich and powerful countries, is an acceptable and realistic way of making other people safe.

It is part of our human condition to be vulnerable, both to our ecosystem and to each other – which is why compassion, based on empathy, is such an essential human quality. It can best be expressed in creating a culture of care and cooperation, which will give rise to the kind of relationships and systems that will make us as secure as we can be. Peacebuilding really is the only way of preventing violence.

Is humanity capable of that?

Nature and nurture

War and human nature

It is often argued that, while the aspirations of those who would end war are noble, they are wholly unrealistic. There have always been wars and always will be. 'Human nature' makes that inevitable.

There have not always been wars. According to archaeological anthropologists such as Brian Ferguson (2003) and Raymond Kelly (2000), systematic, large-scale violence began to take place relatively recently in the long life of our species, and then at different epochs in different parts of the world, according to the circumstances, culture and organisation of societies, as they grew more centralised and less fluid in their boundaries.

That is not to say of course that in times and societies where there was no war no acts of violence were committed, or that violent capacities are not part of the evolutionary inheritance of our species. It is to say that the established institution of systematic warfare and killing on a grand scale are not a necessary outcome of our evolutionary genetic inheritance, and that societies can be relatively very peaceful as well as relatively very violent.

In our own time, while there certainly are societies where direct violence is all too prevalent, in many countries people have only a very small chance of being killed by others living there. While all human beings are capable of both aggression and tenderness, our patterns of behaviour change with norms and circumstances. That in turn means that they are capable of change. It is perfectly possible to have capacities that we do not exercise (or not without restraint), however strong they are, and others that we work hard to develop and use – whether because of our own values or in response to social conditioning and systems that make them desirable. Though we all have the capacity to kill, most of us will never do it; and most of us know that we will be safer if we steer clear of violence, even when threatened by it. We will either hide, run or use our social skills to defuse hostility. At the political level, military powers go to war only when they choose to do so, after careful calculation – not as an act of passion, though possibly in response to popular pressure.

With the sensationally popular publication of Desmond Morris's *The Naked Ape* in 1967 and Richard Dawkins's *The Selfish Gene* a decade later (1976), there was for a while a steady flow of scientific literature that emphasised the idea of innately selfish human brutishness.[4] But this gloomy, determinist view overlooks the other aspects of human nature that prompt us to behave altruistically, to care and be kind, to cooperate for our own benefit and that of others. In more recent scientific writing (see, for instance, de Waal, 1997), our moral sense is emphasised and the success of our species is attributed above all to our social skills, to moral impulses such as

---

4   Dawkins's argument was not in fact about human selfishness but about the genetic selection process, but in popular thinking and discourse the two ideas were conflated.

altruism, respect and compassion, and to the desire to be seen, by ourselves and others, to have done right.

The cultural aspect of our formation is increased by the fact that human beings, unlike other species with which they might be compared, are born completely helpless and remain highly dependent for years rather than weeks or months. This expands the social and cultural component of who and what they become, as compared with their genetic inheritance.

From this scientific viewpoint, the institution of war is a product not of genes but of culture, and it is to culture that I will turn next.

The culture of war

The culture of war is based on the eat-or-be-eaten approach to life alluded to earlier and to consequent dominatory, hierarchical systems and relationships. It is very closely related to the way in which gender is most often constructed: a way that is deeply detrimental to the wellbeing of men and women alike. Again, this has not been true in all times and places, so cannot be regarded as biologically determined. Riane Eisler (1990) has described past societies in which men and women were equal, and this both shaped and reflected the unwarlike and predominantly cooperative and egalitarian cultures in which they lived.

Nevertheless, artefacts around the world represent men as victor-heroes, displaying the will and capacity for dominance, especially as achieved by swords, spears or guns. In recent times some monuments and images display the tragedy of the fallen, but victors have pride of place, most notably in European city centres, where men on powerful horses brandish swords triumphantly. The message they carry is that might is right, strong is good. It is not a man's job to be a loser, especially if he is a leader.

In this model of power, being a leader is in itself manly. Hierarchical relationships are essential to patriarchy, which means, literally, a system in which the father or oldest male in a family is its head. This is the basis of the hierarchical system of male dominance which gives the word its wider meaning. Men are born to be in the controlling seat in the family, in clans, tribes and countries, in places of work, and, of course, in religion. 'Real men' seek dominance over women, first and foremost, and over other men. The power they exercise may be intellectual, emotional or economic, but physical prowess remains emblematic of manhood and all too often is expressed as violence. Domestic violence is endemic, in varying degrees, in most if not all societies. In many places it is still acceptable. Women can be violent too, especially against children, in cultures where that is seen as acceptable, but most domestic violence is inflicted by men, who are often culturally encouraged to uphold their authority in this way. This model of power is based on bullying. Mercifully, some societies are coming to see it that way.

Boys and young men are under pressure from a very early age to conform to macho ideals. They are told that 'big boys don't cry', expected to be tough, and laughed at or applauded for behaviour that in girls would be seen as unkind. By their teens these norms are well established and the pressure to 'step up' is unrelenting. In some societies traditional initiation rites make a direct link between manhood and warfare, while in many cities teenage boys are drawn into gang violence and sometimes into fully fledged gang warfare. Meanwhile states look to young men, overwhelmingly, for army recruitment. In all too many countries, minors are also enlisted. That includes the UK, where children in schools are subjected to military propaganda, involved in cadet corps and prepared for recruitment.[5]

Within this macho culture, sexual acts become a sign of male potency, which is why that word has acquired sexual connotations and rape is often committed as an instrument of war: a demonstration of dominance not only over the women who are violated, but also over the men associated with them, who are regarded as their owners. Rape is also used by men against other men, as a violent act to demonstrate dominance.

In recent years women have been recruited into armies in different parts of the world – sometimes as fighters, but often in support roles

---

5   See https://www.gov.uk/government/news/armed-forces-learning and go to www.forceswatch.net/ [both accessed 29 December 2014]. Recruitment in the UK starts at 16 years of age. For the first year recruits undergo military training, but from the age of 17 they can be involved in active combat. Recruits below the age of 18 need the permission of a parent or guardian to enlist.

– and in practice subjected to discrimination and abuse of different kinds. Overwhelmingly, still, the most usual roles assigned to women in relation to war are those of wives and mothers of fighters, cheering them on and keeping the home fires burning. Alas, along with other noncombatants, they too become war's victims.

In some societies, paradoxically, women are also expected to halt the violence that flares up between their menfolk. Naga women, for instance, living in one of the tribal societies of north-east India, will rush to a scene of fighting, interpose themselves between the warring sides and broker a ceasefire between them. Yet they are excluded from tribal decision making and representation.

Many women are complicit in the ongoing process of creating these patriarchal norms in families, consciously or unconsciously encouraging their children to comply with them. And many men, for reasons of personality or by conscious choice, do not act out their masculinity in the ways required by this macho culture. Increasingly, too, in some societies at least, women are stepping out of traditional womanly roles and behaviour. But deep assumptions, prejudices and pressures remain. Practical caring and nurturing remain largely female roles and are seriously undervalued. Service to others is seen as powerlessness. Similarly, in a hierarchical culture 'career progression' in any form of work is important to status.

The world of politics, certainly in the UK, is an adversarial world in which government and opposition attack and seek to humiliate each other, with the applause of onlookers. The braying to be heard in the House of Commons is a tragicomical performance of masculinity.

When women step into places traditionally reserved for men, they are entering the male world and must perform their roles accordingly if they want to climb the ladder. Golda Meir, Indira Gandhi and Margaret Thatcher were among the first female heads of state and were famous for their 'strong leadership', which included ordering acts of violence at home or abroad.

Taking a country into war is still regarded as a sign of true leadership, at least in the UK. Winston Churchill, whose peacetime leadership was less than successful, achieved the status of national hero in World War II, and subsequent prime ministers have sought to make their mark by going to war. Soldiers represented as war heroes feature frequently in the news, and Help for Heroes ('heroes' meaning 'those maimed in war') rapidly became a top charity in the UK. Thus society daily reinforces the assumption that fighting for one's country (or tribe, or clan, or faction) is a noble thing to do.

Men are no more born to kill than women are. Soldiers, whether male or female, need to be brutalised by initiation rights and military training in order to perform their designated roles. Killing fellow human beings does not come easily and is possible only when empathy is stifled. In his remarkable book *Humanity* (2001), Jonathan Glover tells the story of a man who could not obey an order to shoot a fleeing man, because that man's trousers were falling down. The surge of fellow feeling he experienced was powerful enough to render him incapable of obeying orders.

Warfare does immense psychological damage to combatants. More US soldiers killed themselves or murdered others after the Vietnam war than died during the war itself. Research by a US army general found that in war more soldiers went absent without leave because of the death and injury they inflicted on others than on account of witnessing the death of comrades or fear for their own lives (Baum, 2004).

The inhumanity of war must be felt at some level even by those who promote it, since its true nature is often hidden in euphemistic language. For instance, the ministry for war-fighting is the ministry of 'defence'. Violence is often referred to as 'force', but those two words are not synonymous. Force or coercive strength – for instance in the form of restraint – can in some circumstances be used in ways that do good rather than harm to people. It need not violate.

The phrase 'military intervention' is perhaps more honest, but somehow disguises the true nature of what that involves, in a way that 'war' does not. 'Intervention' is a neutral word and does not reveal the large-scale, violent assault that is meant. Similarly, 'strike' to mean 'bomb' makes the action sound quick, neat and tidy, and its combination with 'surgical' carries the benign connotations of therapeutic precision. (It would be alarming indeed to be struck by one's surgeon, let alone blown to bits.) To 'secure' an area means to eliminate all opposition (people) in order to control it. Perhaps most insidiously of all, 'security' has come to refer more often to military apparatus and measures than to the safety and wellbeing of people.

Not only are words used to disguise the true nature of violence but they reinforce the myth of its quasi-magical power. The phrase 'silver bullet' is the modern-day version of 'magic wand'. 'Bullet points' direct us to what is important, focusing our minds for quick grasp and effective action. 'Targets' give us power to advance.

Sadly, stories such as J. R. R. Tolkien's *The Lord of the Rings* and C. S. Lewis's tales of Narnia are powerful allegories that give expression to the idea of war as the final, apocalyptic cleanser of evil (an idea expressed in and nurtured by many religious texts). These tales, which follow in the line of ancient sagas, are much loved, even among Friends. They may be allegories, in which war is a metaphor, but I suggest that they are, nonetheless, expressions of a false belief that evil can be conquered rather than transformed. As Aleksandr Solzhenitsyn exclaims, in *The Gulag Archipelago* (1974):

> If only it were all so simple! If only there were evil people somewhere insidiously committing evil deeds and it were necessary only to separate them from the rest of us and destroy them. But the dividing line between good and evil cuts through the heart of every human being – and who is willing to destroy a piece of his own heart?

Stories can be just as exciting and far more illuminating without the violence and misleading allegory that perpetuates the myth of war's power for good. We need to create a new story of power that tells of our interdependence and liberates us to be the best of who we are; that locates our power in our innate intelligence and sociability rather than in our capacity for aggression; and acknowledges that men and women alike, to be fully human, must be humane. To expect them to kill in the name of the common good is an unreasonable and destructive requirement. The suspense and relief created by epic tales could be found just as well and less damagingly in tales of heroic and dramatic rescue.

Although human beings are capable of cruelty and aggression, kindness also comes naturally to us. The power of our imagination enables our species to feel (and act on) empathy not only for those near to us but also for people far away, once we recognise their humanity (Philips and Taylor, 2009), once we recognise our common humanity. We as Friends see all people as essentially equal and all capable of goodness: 'that of God' that can 'answer' and be answered. It may be hard to imagine in some people, but I am greatly helped by the saying (of uncertain origin) that 'to understand all is to forgive all', and do believe that everyone, however flawed and damaged, has some good in them that can be touched by love. If that is what we truly believe, we must act accordingly, believing that to do so will be for the good of all.

It is the function of faith not to contradict reality but to give a deeper, truer and more powerful understanding of it. I have tried to show, as best I can, that the currently dominant version of truth in relation to war is false and that the apparent foolishness of a radically different viewpoint is indeed wisdom, an empowering truth to which we must testify. Now, in the next section, I want to consider the power we have to translate that wisdom into action whose nature corresponds with a practical and loving vision for the world. I will start with a Quaker understanding of power.

CHAPTER 2

Power for peace

A different understanding of power

Our faith, rooted as it is in a radical form of Christianity (if no longer tied to its theology), is centred in an alternative understanding and experience of power: one that was taken for granted in the first three hundred years of Christian discipleship and shared much later by George Fox and those who joined him.

At the heart of their faith was belief in the good that could be reached, 'answered' or responded to in every person and the equality of all in the eyes of God. Their understanding of power came from a man called Jesus who, like his Jewish forebears, believed that human beings were made 'in the image of God'. 'Children of God' was the way he put it.

He was born a nobody and remained so for the first thirty-or-so years of his life. When he agonised in the desert about the nature of his calling and future ministry, he vigorously rejected the option of creating a worldly kingdom through conquest, and even of performing spectacular miracles to demonstrate his control over natural law, to convince his audience of his credentials.

He chose instead a life not of control but of apparent powerlessness, a life of service – walking from place to place, talking to people, challenging and encouraging them, sharing his vision of human community and showing profound, unconditional care for others, whether in body or spirit. He focused most of his ministry on those rejected and condemned by the society of his time. Yet the power of his words and the way he behaved ('let his life speak') attracted and convinced people in their thousands, as his reputation grew.

In the teachings that were collected in chapters 5, 6 and 7 of Matthew's account, Jesus gives vivid examples of the revolutionary way in which his followers are to assert their autonomy and equality in facing up to the bullying kind of power: by turning the other cheek when struck (like an underling – with the back of someone's hand), thereby inviting their assailant to strike them with their open palm, as an equal (Wink, 1983); giving away their indoor clothes as well as their coat if that was asked for; carrying a Roman soldier's bags for another mile if pressed into service for the statutory one mile – always acting on their own initiative, acting in line with love, with dignified and immediate magnanimity, rather than simply submitting to violence or injustice or reacting in kind.

Jesus's transforming power was unconstrained by fear for his own safety (though he certainly felt it), with the result that his ministry is said to have lasted only three years, ending almost as soon as it had begun. His terrible execution was a poignant example of human vulnerability – and yet he believed that his acceptance of that humiliation and suffering would also be his greatest power to transform, trusting his friends to continue where he had left off. The power of his life and death grew exponentially because he had shared everything with them, assuring them that they would achieve still greater things. And so it was. Their encounter with love, as he had embodied it, had at last transformed them: made them whole persons, able to do things that they had never dreamt of, in the power of the spirit.

George Fox was just such a disciple, sharing that transformative experience, albeit in a different time and place. Whether we came to the experiential truths to which we now testify through the direct Jesus route or through George Fox, or arrived at the same point through a very different journey, we share the experience of transcending love in our own lives and in meeting for worship, and can let its power speak to us and through us. If that love is in us, we must let our lives show it and speak for the power that can answer humanity's condition.

Here are four short examples of this power in action:

A friend of mine was going to be raped. She managed to take the rapist's face between her hands and look at him, asking if he had no one to love him. He dissolved into tears and let her go.

Another friend was walking along a dark road and being followed by a group of young men on the opposite pavement who were laughing and talking about him in a way that frightened him. He crossed the road and approached them, asking if they could tell him the way to the station. They quickly stopped laughing and not only told him the way but took him there themselves.

A psychiatrist I heard about worked in a mental hospital and was called to attend to a patient who had become wild and agitated, to the point where he had been locked into the sports hall and no one dared to approach him. The psychiatrist went onto the balcony above him and called to him to say that he had been asked to come and help but that he was afraid, and he guessed that he, the patient, was afraid too. What could they do? The man immediately calmed down and the psychiatrist went down to meet him and talk with him, and soon was able to accompany him quietly back to his room.

At the end of World War II, the father of Hildegard Mayr (then a child) was at home with his family and expecting that hungry and war-crazed Russian soldiers, who had entered Vienna, driven out the Germans, and were now rampaging through the city, would at any moment come banging at their door ready to loot, kill and rape. He asked his family to go down to the cellar and, when the anticipated banging came, opened the door quietly and told the soldiers that they were welcome to his house, but asked them to leave their guns outside. He explained that if he had their assurance that they would behave with courtesy, his family would be glad to give them a meal. Touched and disarmed by this quiet welcome, the men laid down their weapons and entered the house. The family came up to meet them and they sat down to eat, together.

Remember too the man who was spared because his trousers fell down. His vulnerability, albeit unintended, had saved his life. The moral power of human affinity and empathy is very great. It plays a key role in work for peace at any level. The vulnerability of unarmed actors becomes their greatest strength, because it removes the hostility and sense of moral justification that spring from fear. When I was working as a neighbourhood mediator, our team discovered that often when violence had been at issue it was better to use women mediators with male clients because they were more readily perceived as nonthreatening and their presence discouraged aggression.

That is doubtless why women in some societies are, like the Naga women referred to earlier, expected to come between warring groups of men. Some women who wish to protest against violence choose to be naked when they do it, emphasising their vulnerability and appealing to the human decency of those they are confronting.

In all four of the examples above, the power of those confronting violence lay in what their response communicated. Communication, when it is well judged and emotionally intelligent, is the essence of this form of transformative power, whether it comes through words, images, music or action. It is expressed in caring and healing; challenging and standing up for people and principles with courage and respect; intervening, physically, between people; exercising moral authority to create calm and enable dialogue; facilitating dialogue and accommodation; inspiring, persuading and convincing; using surprise to change the dynamics of interaction; analysing situations in ways that shed new light on the kind of action needed; reframing situations to help others to see them differently; generating creative ideas for problem solving; identifying common ground; negotiating intelligently and respectfully; understanding and coming close enough to others to gain their trust and help them to see themselves differently and transformatively; enabling empathy in others; using story and humour to dissipate fear and free minds and hearts, and symbolic action to move people. (For more on nonviolent power, see Francis, 2002.)

All sorts and conditions of people can exercise this kind of power. It offers a way for individuals to act effectively and morally in response to personal danger and can have great power when used collectively. It is to collective nonviolent action that I will turn next.

Mobilising nonviolent power: stages and processes in conflict transformation

Responding to tyranny

Friends tend to think first of a peacemaker as someone who helps to resolve conflict, the go-between or mediator who offers 'good offices' and is able to empathise with all concerned; who helps them to think constructively, enter into dialogue and reach an accommodation with each other. However, while conflict resolution is a vital part of peacemaking, and mediators can play an important role, in situations where there is gross asymmetry of power and serious oppression or injustice such a process is unlikely to be possible (see the diagram 'Stages and processes in conflict transformation' in the appendix). The power asymmetry will have to be changed first, and that will begin to happen when those suffering the oppression (in whatever context) get some insight into their situation and start talking about it with others so that they build their understanding together. Through this process of awareness raising (which Paolo Freire called 'conscientisation'; Freire, 1972) they can begin to visualise a different state of affairs and to plan what they can do to begin to bring it about.

The essential starting point for all their preparations will be the establishment of shared values, to be reflected both in their vision and in their behaviour. They will need to build their courage and commitment together if they are going to resist or confront the powers that be. They will also need to prepare well for all contingencies and be ready to seize the moment, when it comes, planning how to use their collective solidarity to minimise risk, protect each other and support each others' families in case of serious eventualities.

This kind of collective power for change in the face of seemingly overwhelming power needs to be learned from past experience in countries like those in Latin America where well-organised nonviolent resistance to violent tyranny has taken place. Developing a sound base of knowledge about how to mobilise collective nonviolent power is vital if we are to find or develop serious answers to the 'What about ...?' questions that others ask us and that we must ask ourselves – though we must avoid creating a counter-mythology of power.

There is no magic answer, violent or nonviolent, and since the currently predominating system is a military one, the examples that can be given of other ways of resisting evil are often relatively small in scale and can seem insignificant. I will return to this problem at the end of this section.

Even within the lifetime of many of us, there have been remarkable examples of nonviolent power. Those best known when I was young were the *satyagraha* movement, led by Gandhi to liberate India from British rule (which eventually came to an end in 1947), and the civil rights movement in the USA in the 1960s, led by Martin Luther King and others.

The struggle in South Africa, for freedom from apartheid, had an extended history that began and ended with nonviolence but also had a violent thread. It started in the early 1950s with a nonviolent

African National Congress (ANC), whose leader, Chief Albert Luthuli, won the Nobel Peace Prize. Then, after the massacre at Sharpville in 1960, when police opened fire on black demonstrators outside the police station and killed 69 of them, nonviolent resistance was eclipsed by the armed struggle in which Nelson Mandela was involved.

Nonviolence eventually came into its own again in the massive protests against 'Bantu' education in the townships, followed by the rent boycotts, business boycotts and daily levels of popular protest and resistance. It was this popular resistance in the townships, supported by many deeply committed members of the anti-apartheid movement in the white population, together with the help of international boycotts and diplomatic pressure, that eventually toppled apartheid and, with Mandela playing a key negotiating and reconciling role, paved the way for majority rule. That eventually came in 1994, four years after Mandela's release from gaol.

By then, a dramatic, unarmed revolution had been brought about in the Philippines, where the growing 'people power' demonstrations (resulting from years of preparation in Christian 'base communities' and sparked by the assassination of Benigno or 'Ninoy' Aquino in 1983) culminated in the removal of dictator Ferdinand Marcos in 1986, when his army's pursuit of a defected military unit was blocked by nuns and others offering flowers, food and cigarettes to the tank drivers.

Then, in 1989, the collapse of the Soviet empire began in Central and Eastern Europe, starting in Poland, where the country's first trade union, Solidarity, had been born in 1980 in the shipyards of Gdansk. With support from the Catholic Church it grew into a mass movement of civil resistance to unjust working conditions and one-party rule. The strikes that took place around Poland are just one example of the power of non-cooperation, which can make tyranny, whether that of invasion or of an existing regime, eventually untenable, showing that governance depends on the cooperation of the governed.

A series of almost entirely nonviolent revolutions followed, sweeping from Poland through Hungary, East Germany, Bulgaria, Czechoslovakia, Romania (where the head of state and his wife were, alas, executed, after violent attempts to crush the revolution) and, last, Albania. Soon the collapse of the Soviet Union itself was under way and eventually arrived at the Kremlin. The Union of Soviet Socialist Republics (USSR) formally ceased to exist on 26 December 1991.

Whatever the internal weaknesses and conflicts that underlay the dissolution of the Soviet empire, it was the quiet courage and persistence of protesters that brought it about with so very little violence. Their nonviolent discipline made it hard for police and troops to attack them, and in many instances won them over. This was true also of the eventual nonviolent removal of Slobodan Milosevic from power in Serbia, some time after the terrible wars in what had once been Yugoslavia, when he was refusing to accept eventual electoral defeat.

As I shall discuss later, in many cases where nonviolent people power was used to resist a violent system, it was mixed with other means of resistance. Moreover, the outcomes, though dramatic, were often disappointing in the longer term. In recent years we have had our hopes raised high and then dashed by the 'Arab Spring', which turned, by and large, into a very unpleasant winter in which nonviolence was abandoned when it was met with violence.

There are many lessons to be learned. These tragic events are a reminder of the depth of preparation and degree of unity among a population that are needed for nonviolence on this scale to succeed in achieving the sudden removal of a regime and replacing it with something better. Even in the more successful cases cited above, the liberation that occurred was just a momentous first step along a very hard road. Yet the liberating potential of well-prepared nonviolent action on a sufficient scale is clear, and it has been shown that its success rate is high, when compared with that of military action (Chenoweth and Stephan, 2011).

Protection against victimisation and communal violence

Just as under Nazi occupation Jewish people were given refuge by brave fellow citizens in non-Jewish homes in France and the Netherlands, protective action of this kind has been offered in a wide range of contexts to people being hunted down because of their religious or ethnic identity. In Idi Amin's Uganda, villagers gave refuge in their own homes to neighbours who otherwise would have been killed, and during the wars that broke up Yugoslavia, peace and human rights activists in Osijek (Croatia) hid people whom they regarded as compatriots who were now at risk of murder because of their parentage.

In the Indian state of Orissa, in 2008, activists mobilised public protests against intercommunal violence and worked to build solidarity rather than enmity between different marginalised groups.[6] In Kenya, when deadly violence broke out in certain areas at the time of the 2007 elections, a powerful group of women activists stepped in to broker a political agreement to bring it to an end[7] and since then many steps have been taken at the community level to build bridges of solidarity, address grievances and prevent recurrences of violent behaviour.[8]

In repressive situations where to speak out is to risk detention or disappearance, the presence of nonviolent accompaniers (such as those who worked for Peace Brigades International in Guatemala) can make all the difference, especially when supported by human rights organisations, which will give international publicity to any acts of violence by the state.

In circumstances where larger scale violence-prevention or peacekeeping roles are needed, they can be undertaken by civilian monitors or police, with the support of local people. Of course, resources on the scale of those given to armies are not currently available for the training and deployment of civilian peace-makers and keepers, but their potential is enormous. In many situations, the sheer fact of being known to be unarmed, and therefore nonthreatening and indeed vulnerable, is powerfully disarming psychologically, as demonstrated in the small examples I gave earlier.

---

6 I received details of this demonstration in 2008 in a letter from a personal friend, who works to build bridges between two oppressed groups in Orissa.

7 www.berghof-handbook.net/documents/publications/dialogue6_dekha_comm.pdf [accessed 29 December 2014]. *The Berghof Handbook for Conflict Transformation* offers a continuously updated online platform for both academics and practitioners to discuss new ideas and exchange experiences in the field of conflict transformation.

8 On support from British Quakers for nonviolent action by Kenyan Quakers, see Chico (2010).

I remember that a Friend at Oxford St Giles Meeting, greatly exercised by the carnage of the Vietnam war, wanted to create a citizens' initiative to take an unarmed 'army' there to intervene. His idea seemed both mad and right. Its madness lay in its novelty and the fact that it was so unlikely that anyone would take it seriously – even Friends. Yet, given the necessary logistical support and resources, and the brave souls to volunteer, I believe it would have been at least as sane as any other kind of intervention. Nonviolent intervention works for Naga women, so why not for brave others? It is accepted that soldiers risk their lives, and there are civilian workers who do so too, whether to rescue people from earthquakes or to nurse people with deadly diseases.

It is possible to imagine circumstances of immediate violence in which coercive force of some kind might be feasible and could be judged necessary to immobilise those carrying out acts of violence without harming them, particularly while guns are still in circulation. Research and development could be undertaken to explore this possibility and create the necessary capability. Such measures are already taken sometimes, for compassionate purposes, in relation to animals of other species than ours, without inflicting the suffering associated with current police immobilisation techniques (such as the use of tasers). If they inflicted no harm or suffering, they might offer a means of swift intervention in exceptional circumstances where someone has become deranged, or in chaotic situations where shooting to wound or kill (let alone bombing) would inflict more deaths and be effectively indiscriminate.

However, such coercion, though not violent in outcome, carries the energy of violence and is liable to drive immediate or future violent responses. There would also be the risk of misuse of such powers and a question of lawful authority. Far more important and transformative will be research, simulations and experiments devoted to discovering more about what makes nonviolent and noncoercive interventions work, building on existing experience. We already know that vulnerability that is freely chosen can disarm people who are about to behave, or are behaving, violently, and that empathic communication can establish human connections and appeal to moral sensibilities.

I am convinced that there is much to be learned from the best of policing (and indeed from the worst). Police personnel can show extreme patience and skill when dealing with deranged and violent individuals, and encouraging work has been done to study the relative efficacy of police forces, as compared with armies, to contain and reduce violence in much broader violent contexts (Harris, 2004). All those who are experienced in nonviolent intervention of different kinds will have much to offer. There can, however, be no doubt that courage is needed to confront violence nonviolently, and it calls for a level of inner calm that may not be needed for fighting.

Whatever the context, specific acts of protest and resistance are only steps in an ongoing process. For instance, the work of Ekta Parishad in India (which Friends have supported through Quaker Peace & Social Witness) has involved campaigns for justice for the poor for more than twenty years and involves eleven thousand community-based organisations in eleven states. It not only mobilises villagers across the country in a remarkable way but engages in dialogue with government at the state and national level. Ekta Parishad's massive, month-long marches have won a series of concessions and changes from the Indian government.[9]

Overcoming the violence of injustice and transforming lives may prove the work of more than one lifetime. Especially when a dramatic form of change is aimed for, it will call for more than the assertive energy and demands of resisters. To bring about a genuinely nonviolent outcome the process of change will need to be inclusive in its vision and aim, and dialogical as well as declamatory in its conduct. If a new form of tyranny is not to replace the old, assertiveness needs to be exercised in a way that does not block the way to eventual resolution. It may well be necessary to exercise patience and give time for social accommodation and consolidation before further progress can be made, even when power disparities have been addressed. And since any movement is likely to be, in reality, a movement of movements, it is important for the spirit and skills of accommodation and conflict resolution to be in operation also within it.

---

9   See http://www.ektaparishad.com/en-us/about/history.aspx [accessed 30 December 2014].

De-escalation and dialogue

The aim of any campaign of nonviolence (which by definition is inclusive in its values) must be to reach a just outcome for all those affected. Although the search for such an outcome to conflict is highly unlikely to bear fruit when power relations are grossly asymmetrical, if mobilisation can shift them so that the campaign wins some recognition from the powers that be, dialogue, always on offer from the side of the campaigners, is increasingly likely to be accepted, so that a process of negotiation can begin.

Moreover, many conflicts do not fit the 'oppressor versus oppressed' model that we tend to associate with nonviolent resistance. In times of turbulence and rapid change, suppressed identities may have assumed new importance (as they did in the former Soviet and Yugoslav countries), all too often with the help of politicians who foment division and fuel anger in order to create a leadership role for themselves and build their popular power.

Often it is other factors – economic pressure, scarcity or high prices when households are already struggling, or political uncertainty, for instance – that have brought people into tension with each other. Sometimes there is a genuine clash of interests between one group and another that can lead to counterproductive and damaging action, rather than being addressed through a process of negotiation and accommodation. Acts of violence in such contexts are like matches thrown into a powder keg. Once violence has taken place the process of polarisation can be very rapid, making communication increasingly difficult and indeed dangerous for individuals who refuse to take sides. Even without the difficulty of power disparity, creating the will for dialogue may still be very difficult.

Nevertheless, effective nonviolent action can be taken and can succeed. In the Wajir district of pastoralist north-east Kenya, at a time of severe drought, desperation and displacement in the region, inter-clan violence had escalated and spread, creating a state of acute fear and mistrust in which normal life was paralysed. A group of women, seeing that their usual market trading had become impossible, got together and began a wider conversation between the women in their marketplace, and ten women were chosen to ensure that peaceful trading could be resumed. Encouraged by this success and by the approval of the local authority, the women decided to go and talk to the clan elders who could influence the wider violence in a highly patriarchal society. They wisely identified one venerable elder of a small clan with little vested interest in the conflict, who would have the trust and respect of other elders, and he used his standing to challenge the rest with the destructiveness of their current behaviour and the need to end the violence. He (again, wisely) appealed to their courage and sense of responsibility, and each clan accepted the challenge and appointed a team of men who would monitor and guide affairs within their own clan or group of clans. Each group of elders was given an egg to keep safe, as a symbol of the fragility and preciousness of peace, and through the courageous interventions of the monitoring teams the violence was eventually brought to an end.[10]

There are many remarkable individuals, community groups and civil society organisations around the world that are working to defuse tensions and build more constructive relationships or to rebuild the capacity for coexistence where violence has taken place. In all such situations, building communication to avoid or overcome polarisation is essential, since any violence can quickly escalate. Promoting dialogue means generating a spirit of outreach and creating safe opportunities for the kind of exchange that builds empathy within and between communities.

Achieving inclusive resolution

For intermediaries to help in the search for a genuine, mutually acceptable and inclusive resolution of conflict, they will need to exercise the 'powerless' kind of power. If the agreement that is reached is to receive the people's mandate and to last, it must be created and owned by the parties to the conflict. It must therefore be mediated by genuine facilitators, not 'power mediators' who want to impose their solution. The facilitators will need to have the trust of both or all parties and at all times to treat them with equal respect. The trust and moral authority they are given will enable them to

---

10 The film *The Wajir Story* (an initiative of Responding to Conflict) is available at the time of writing to watch online at www.youtube.com/watch?v=Y1dzs16Heh0. Notes accompanying the film can be downloaded at http://www.respond.org/data/files/LPP_video_notes/lpp_wajir_story_video_notes.pdf [both sites accessed 30 December 2014].

establish the 'ground rules' that are necessary to enable a respectful and productive conversation to take place, and the facilitators will need to hold the parties to them.

In addition to assisting the process of constructive dialogue, or rather as one form of support for it, intermediaries can offer their care, understanding and commitment to the conflicting parties: qualities that are needed as much by those who have committed acts of violence as by those who have not. Some years ago I worked with a paramilitary group in Northern Ireland that had decided to demilitarise. During that experience I came to see and feel that when violence, damaging as that is to both perpetrator and victim, has become your way of life, the source of your income, your friendships, your status and your very identity, it is very hard – even in your imagination – to step into a radically different, unknown place. For you, this is likely to be as frightening as any step you have ever taken.

Northern Ireland offers an example of the complexity of peace processes, and also of their longevity, which is related to the length of time it took for British politicians to decide to hold serious talks with key players in the violence. However, it also offers an example of the positive role of community work to keep on doggedly rebuilding community relationships and prepare the ground for peace 'at the top'. It shows too that, even once a settlement has been reached and is more or less acceptable to most people, there are likely still to be others who remain disaffected and scarred by the past. It is therefore important to deal as constructively as possible with the damage that remains.

Demilitarisation and dealing with the past

Once a settlement has been reached after armed violence, a process of disarmament, demobilisation and reintegration (DDR) is needed, in order to build a secure peace for the future. However, more often than not that concept is applied to non-state-armed groups only, rather than to state armies as well, and erstwhile 'insurgents' are often integrated into a state's armed forces or police. (This partial approach to demilitarisation is of course related to the much wider notion of the nation state as a military unit that has the monopoly of violence.)

Not only does civilian life need to be restored, but, when conflict has taken a violent course, there will be a great deal of emotional scarring that is left, both social and personal. Dealing with the past (known as DWP) will be a long and difficult journey, and will need to be multilayered. While the truth of what happened to people can sometimes be established empirically (for instance through the discovery and identification of remains in particular places, or multiple reliable eye-witness accounts), the broader account and interpretation of events are liable to remain contested. However, those different accounts need to be heard and acknowledged.

How to award 'justice' is then a matter of potentially inexhaustible debate. Who is to be held to account when a very high proportion of the population has been involved in one way or another and victims are also sometimes perpetrators, and vice versa. Then, is the idea to punish, or to mitigate the pain and loss of what was done and the hatred that it has engendered?

While in some societies the focus is on punishment, within many traditional justice systems the aim is to redress loss and heal feelings and relationships, as far as is humanly possible. Post-apartheid South Africa, through the work of the Truth and Reconciliation Commission led by Desmond Tutu, pioneered a serious attempt to hold together the goal of bringing some sense of completion to victims through disclosure of what happened and holding perpetrators to account when they did not come forward and cooperate with the Commission's work.

In some societies, members of a community who have committed a crime know that if they confess, acknowledge and apologise for their crime and the harm it has caused, and then carry out symbolic acts of purification and make whatever reparation is possible, they will be accepted back into their community. This has happened for instance with child soldiers in Northern Uganda who have committed atrocities and often returned home hardened and unrepentant. Through the patient, self-giving work of community members, healing has at last been achieved.

The purpose of such processes is to enable the social fabric to be restored and all concerned to move forward together. I believe it has much to teach us. It requires a deep spirit of generosity. We in the UK know this approach as 'restorative justice', and it is gradually gaining currency here, as it is in some other 'modern' societies.

There are many experimental ways in which local communities contribute to dealing with the past. One example comes from the Centre for Nonviolent Action, based in Belgrade, which is working with former combatants from different sides in the Yugoslav wars to face, first together and then publicly in their communities, the loss and suffering caused on all sides by the fighting in which they took part.

Another example is a recently launched project of small groups of individuals in Abkhazia and Georgia. Although their governments are still in a relationship of hostility, they have begun to work in parallel on a 'memory project' that will try to gather eye-witness accounts of events as they were experienced at the personal level, to give recognition to all who suffered and to create the basis for learning from the past in order to build a better future.

For the sake of that future, it is vital to establish a social and political culture in which conflict, when it happens, is approached constructively: regarded not as a signal for aggressive or violent behaviour but as something that can be addressed through dialogue and negotiation, so that mutually acceptable ways forward can be found. Even in the most humdrum of individual daily lives, conflicts arise. After major violent upheavals, in complex societies and in a constantly changing global context, there will be conflicts of all kinds to be addressed and a continuing need for accommodation and change within relationships.

Governments and geopolitics: the contrast between potential and reality

I tend to think of peacemaking in terms of what can be done for peace at the community level and by civil society organisations, and that is reflected in what I have written above. It is partly because that is what I know best and partly because so much truly constructive work is in fact done at these levels; but of course the policies and actions of governments have immense impact.

Genuinely participatory and inclusive systems of governance are necessary to a positive, lasting peace in any country: governance that is exercised accountably and in the spirit of service to all sectors of society. Good governance can provide the political stability necessary for the development of norms and systems within which the injustices and conflicts that will inevitably arise in any society can be addressed without damaging disruption or violence.

When governments are imposed on populations, whether by interference from outside or internal tyranny, the prospects for just and lasting peace are bleak. External governments and intergovernmental organisations, given the will, could do much more to support local peace initiatives (without using them for their own purposes) and encourage and support positive change at the governmental level. They can also exercise influence through nonmilitary sanctions, if asked to do so by a popular movement, though these can strengthen the resistance of a regime, and even support for it, as well as having a sometimes devastating effect on ordinary people. Incentives are in general more effective (see *Incentives, sanctions and conditionality in peacemaking*, 2008).

To have legitimacy and make a lastingly constructive contribution, any supportive intervention from outside needs to come from a truly disinterested third party. Whether a mediating team is composed of independent individuals or of representatives of a national or international organisation or government, true mediators (like those Norwegians who facilitated the process leading to the Oslo Agreement) can play an important role in changing the dynamics of a conflict and preventing or addressing violence.

Alas, examples of such constructive governmental roles are eclipsed by those of inflammatory intervention and 'power mediation', whose goal is to dictate the terms of a process and agreement in line with external agendas, rather than to enable the parties to the conflict to reach a mutually acceptable outcome. Earlier, I outlined the course and fate of 'diplomatic' action in relation to Kosovo (see above, 'Humanitarian wars', p. 25), and will now offer two (more recent) examples of the way potentially constructive responses to violent conflict have been displaced by hegemonic politics and military action.

Not only in Libya but in North Africa and the Middle East at large, the instability and violence are extreme, with global military powers desperately pursuing their own regional interests. The tragic events in Gaza and the continued shrinking of the space left for an eventual Palestinian state, coupled with the isolation of a belligerent Israel, are inextricably linked with the wider violent instability in the region. This includes the terrible, multisided war in Syria and the new wave of deadly violence in Iraq, which now involves Islamic State (IS) fighters. They have been joined locally by disaffected Sunnis who, since the toppling of Saddam Hussein and the purging of other Sunni politicians and civil servants (which was promoted by the West), have continued to be marginalised by the Iraqi government.

Barack Obama's description of IS as a 'network of death' was not in itself inaccurate but it seemed to miss the point that the US itself leads just such a network, in which the UK is an active participant. It is not this violent group or that which threatens us all, but the toxic combination of spiralling violence and counter-violence, fuelled by different forms of militarist ideology; and it is the superpowers that have the capacity to destroy the globe.

The beheading of Western hostages (the first of them in a month in which Saudi Arabia, a Western ally equipped with arms from the UK among others, publicly beheaded 19 people) has brought more promises of retributive violence from the West. There seems to be no recognition that blowing people limb from limb – whether on purpose or as predictable 'collateral damage' – is equally lacking in compassion, or that the 'war on terror' and almost incessant military intervention in the region have made a massive contribution to hatred and chaos. (And is ghoulish boastfulness about violence morally worse than euphemisms?)

The violence of those who pervert Islam will not be stopped by counter-violence. Indeed, it has grown in response to it. Those who perpetrate it would argue that they are avenging the arrogance and violence of the West. However unlikely or even impossible they may seem at present, dialogue and understanding are the only things that can dissolve extremism of any kind. They need to be put at the centre of policy now and pursued at every level. Those local people who are working for peace, against all the odds, need to be supported – not constantly disrupted or overwhelmed by the actions of big powers.

The current crisis within Ukraine and in relations between the

West and Russia (which continues to unfold as I write and no doubt will have changed again by the time this is read) resulted not only from divisions within Ukraine itself but from years of geopolitical contest between the West and Russia, which, despite initial thawing in the immediate aftermath of the collapse of the Soviet Union, has continued to varying degrees since the Cold War in theory ended.

Many of the countries that had been part of the former Soviet empire in Eastern Europe, having escaped its repression and hastened its collapse, sought NATO membership and were welcomed in. This must have been a bitter pill for proud, nationalist Russia to swallow, resulting as it did in the expansion right up to its borders of an organisation that was formed to confront Soviet communism and might have been expected to disband once the Cold War was over. At the same time, in addition to its loss of political influence, Russia lost important trading and economic power to the European Union. Yet within former Soviet countries like Ukraine, Moldova and Georgia, although governments were turning to the West, there remained substantial regional populations that still looked to Russia – politically, culturally and economically. They felt alienated from West-leaning governments and their supporters, and wanted be recognised for themselves and to remain close to Russia.

This was the background against which the West and Russia responded to the 'Euromaidan' protest in Kyiv (which, like the earlier 'Orange Revolution', was supported by the USA). Many people across the country were tired of the kleptocratic government then in power in Kyiv and backed the protest at the beginning. However, another key factor in sparking the revolution was the offer of associate status with the European Union, when a significant part of the population was not ready for such a lasting divisive realignment.

And so the protest, step by rapid step, turned into a political struggle between the old industrial East, with its predominantly Russian-speaking and Russia-leaning population, and the Europhiles in Kyiv and the West of Ukraine, with both Russia and the Western allies treating the contest as a continuation of their struggle for regional influence and playing their roles accordingly, on both sides fanning rather than dampening the flames. Russia's swift move to annex Crimea fuelled the conflict within Ukraine and infuriated the West, while the West's approach to 'talks' was so biased that it did little to enable real dialogue and much to encourage Russian isolation and defiance. More than three thousand deaths have so far resulted.

The impact of this violence has been felt elsewhere in the region. I know that the work of Georgian and Abkhazian bridgebuilders has been made more difficult than ever by the hardened attitudes of their governments, and the tensions between the NATO countries and Russia, intensified by military manoeuvres, threaten a new Cold War.

As I write, there are signs that there may be a pulling back from the brink, in the light of the ever-growing violence in the Middle East. Perhaps now the will can be generated to initiate what was needed from the start: genuinely open dialogue within Ukraine to seek some form of local and national resolution. That could involve, for instance, greater devolution of powers to a relatively autonomous eastern Ukraine and trading arrangements that include both Russia and Europe. I sincerely hope that space will be made for citizens' peace initiatives on the ground to contribute to and support some such accommodation.

I have given these complex regional conflicts some focus in order to illustrate the fact that substantial and lasting transformation cannot be achieved unless local conflicts are seen as part of a wider picture. They do not happen in isolation from other, wider ones and actions at one level are affected by those at another.

Therefore, for now, we cannot simply point to heartening examples of nonviolent conflict transformation on the national and international scale to prove what is possible. We have to recognise that for those examples to be created and at last to become the norm, a radical change will be needed in mainstream thinking about power and the role of the nation state, and in approaches to international relations: a change that abandons the pursuit of security by contest and embraces the praxis of common security.

CHAPTER 3

Agenda for transformation

What needs to be transformed

Our whole system of global relationships, political and economic, is inimical to peace. Until the global body politic can overcome its addiction to contest and belief in military alliances and 'solutions', the kind of behaviour outlined above will continue to disrupt the work of peacemaking and cooperation, and prevent us from addressing the urgent and profound problems that we all face.

At the same time, experience of practical peacemaking in social and political conflict has generated much-needed expertise on what can be done to transform these currently destructive relationships and responses. Indeed, experience of day-to-day life and of neighbourhood or domestic peacemaking furnishes much knowledge of the human dynamics involved in managing conflicts constructively.

The work that citizens undertake for peace, sometimes in the face of extreme violence, is as inspiring as it is vital. It undoubtedly saves lives, creates space for dialogue and changes relationships. Sadly, however, it is all too often interrupted and thwarted. The apparently boundless desire of the big military powers to retain and extend their geopolitical spheres of control and access to resources is like a great, relentless tide that brings constant reversals and robs local people of the agency that should be theirs.

It is hard for peace to be made 'on the ground' when the unseen hand of a superpower is manipulating events in line with a different agenda and arms dealers are stoking the fire of local animosities and power struggles. Arms traders, governments and insurgents all find ways of funding and acquiring the means to make money and kill, while local peacebuilders struggle to find funds for saving lives. The resources made available to support civilian work for peace are minute in comparison to those devoted to capacities for armed violence.

The dominant agenda of many governments is to act in 'the national interest' and what is described as security, rather than for the wider good. It is at odds with the principle of global responsibility, which is fundamental to future peace and human security. It creates a competitive and conflictual dynamic that in turn serves and is fuelled by the arms industry. Given the histories from which most governments have emerged, they are not often far-sighted enough to see that it is in everyone's interest to build a better, safer, fairer and more sustainable world. At least, they may see it sometimes, to a degree, but the political dynamics of which they are part, and perhaps a selfish electorate, tend to overwhelm that insight.[11]

The very way in which states are defined, as units of military control, is inimical to peace and security. 'Territorial integrity' is irrelevant to most things that really affect our wellbeing. State boundaries do not curtail the movement of weapons, any more than they control the weather, and since they have been determined in more or less arbitrary ways, through adventures and accidents of history (usually military ones), they present a potentially endless source of conflict without conferring any real benefit on the people contained within them. They incorporate people in units where they feel they do not belong while excluding others who have been forced by war or poverty to migrate, and long to find a home in them.

States are not alone as units of defence and attack, but the threat and use of violence, whether in the name of national and allied interests or of group identity or ideology (religious or secular), is the cause of the carnage and destruction of war. It cannot be the solution. Hegemonic agendas can cause the destruction of villages and towns, countries and regions. They threaten our entire world.

The realpolitik that justifies such agendas is not 'real' in the sense of offering sound analysis and good guidance. We can see its outcomes all around us. It has not created anything approximating to justice or security for people or planet. It is not to be equated with wisdom of any kind, let alone the wisdom that comes from God or the spirit, the guide deep within. It is the false wisdom that has created a world awash with weapons and an economy fuelling and fuelled by the cycle of violence.

---

11 The Brandt Commission report, which some of us will remember, still shines from the past like a beacon because its writers did see and present fairness in global economics as a matter not only of ethics but of common interest. http://www.odi.org/sites/odi.org.uk/files/odi-assets/publications-opinion-files/6638.pdf [accessed 30 December 2014].

First Dog on the Moon 2014, by Andrew Marlton.

The relentlessly spiralling arms race adds ever-more-sophisticated weapons to the arsenals of those who can afford and control them. Drones are proliferating, being under development in many countries, including for instance Iran and China. They and 'precision' bombing not only kill a great many more civilians than their advocates claim, but also offer the users the option of launching deadly violence without physical risk to their own side (though the psychological harm to those who commit these distance atrocities is severe) (Dao, 2013). Such 'capabilities' make warfare all too easy for those who possess them but cataclysmic for those on the receiving end.

Meanwhile cyber warfare is already underway, generating new nightmares of deadly chaos (the UK Government announced a National Offensive Cyber Programme in Autumn 2013)[12] and opening up a new battleground that could drive the rest. Perhaps most seriously of all, the risk of nuclear catastrophe, though largely forgotten, has not gone away but, together with climate change,

---

12 See *A Strong Britain in the Age of Uncertainty* (2010). See also the extended interview with Edward Snowden at http://www.wired.com/2014/08/edward-snowden/ [accessed 30 December 2014].

threatens our entire planet (see Rogers, 2012).

All this when the shame of grinding poverty, hunger, disease and illiteracy continue; when, time after time, the 'international community' fails to respond in any adequate way to the plight of those affected by catastrophes of one kind and another, ready to drop bombs but not to see that refugee children are educated or to give them safe homes away from violence; when climate change, whose impact on the most vulnerable is already deadly, has not begun to be addressed in any serious way and ecological degradation continues.

All these are ills that war not only fails to address but exacerbates. Militarism has had long enough to prove itself and it has done so only too well. The results are there for all to see. Yet the very extremity of the violence it has generated has caught us in its embrace and makes it hard for us to gather our resolve and finally turn away from it. It is the embodiment of the greatest evil we could ever imagine, yet its huge compass makes it hard for us to see the sky or to feel the moral ground beneath our feet.

What kind of faith offers nothing beyond this? We need to see the possibility of a radically different way of coexisting and to act to help bring it into being, in the knowledge that love is the greatest power of all and that all human beings are capable of it. Common security is the best we can ever have, both morally and practically.

The age of militarism must be brought to a close. For Friends, it is a matter of integrity and authenticity that we commit ourselves to that goal, as a Society, heart, mind and soul, supporting each other in faith. We must accept that we will not always have answers and that sometimes we will find ourselves, and others, helpless to prevent some great suffering. But we can be sure that to contribute to the demilitarisation of human society and an increase in human kindness is the surest and greatest way in which we can reduce the suffering caused by violence, both now and in the future.

The changes that are needed

If nonviolent, constructive ways of building just and peaceful relationships are to be given the chance to create the highest degree of security possible in a fragile and unpredictable world, everything that has been learned from local work to transform violent conflict must be applied with equal urgency to the militarised global context. The theory and stories that have emerged from local experience must somehow be translated into radically new thinking about what makes for human security, and from there into mainstream policy and resources for the transformation of international relationships and systems.

We need not 'foreign policy' but policy for a genuinely internationalist approach to international relations. That policy must be based on the principles of mutual respect and care, and supported by a radical shift in public understanding both of what is right and what makes for security and wellbeing. It will need to be applied not only in different kinds of interpersonal and intersocietal relationship but also in the building of truly international structures for the cooperative exercise of shared responsibility.

Just, caring and participatory systems of governance will need to be developed by each society for itself and cooperatively between societies, to regulate the relationship between them. A radically reformed, egalitarian United Nations – or some equivalent international body – will be needed as a forum for cooperation, mutual guidance and support: a place in which moral leadership can be exercised and agreements reached, policy shaped and solidarity built – and all in favour of just economic relationships, the upholding of human rights and responsibilities, and the healing of our ecosystem. Nonviolent forms of dispute resolution will be a taken-for-granted expression of the mutual respect that binds the whole system, underpins its values and gives it its resilience.

One important aspect and outcome of these changes will be increasing permeability and cooperation between different units of governance – local, national, regional and international. The state will be a unit of operation and cooperation, instead of a unit to defend; its boundaries a matter of mutual convenience rather than contested principle.

Since relationships of deep hostility currently exist between different nations, alliances, identities and ideologies, there will be a long way to go before such a transformation, or something like it, can begin to get under way. A great deal of conciliation work will be needed, and serious restorative processes to heal or dissolve the effects of past injury and suffering, suspicion and humiliation. Where violent hostilities between different groups and nations are currently beyond control, and attempts at resolution have so far failed, tireless efforts will be necessary to support and encourage the achievement of ceasefires, dialogue and eventual just and inclusive settlements, so that the long road to peace can begin.

At every level and in every sphere, peace will need to be understood not simply as the absence of war but as a state of positive, cooperative living together that embraces equality, justice, and care for each other and the global ecology of which we are part. It will involve respecting human rights and accepting the responsibilities that they imply; participatory ways of conducting *res publica* or public affairs; fair access to and sustainable use of resources; constructive relationships between different sectors of society; and a united will to create a radically new and caring relationship with the rest of our ecosystem.

Within and between one society or community and another there will be different understandings of some aspects of human rights and the meaning of equality. For instance, there are deep cultural divisions over gender and sexuality. For most if not all readers of this book, it will be quite clear that equality encompasses both of these aspects of human living and that all human beings have the right to express themselves in roles, relationships and behaviour that is guided by love and respect. Yet many people still adhere to dominant narratives within their cultures that make them see things very differently.

There will be many difficult conversations ahead, and 'nonviolent insistence' will be a necessary adjunct to respectful listening. However, I am certain that through loving and persistent dialogue change will surely come.

As peace in all these aspects is being built, a thoroughgoing process of practical demilitarisation will be needed to accompany the dissolving of enmity and demilitarisation of thinking that are taking place: first of all a process of disarmament of all kinds, in a programme that eventually 'puts beyond use' everything from small arms to nuclear weapons. The research, development, production and trading that are currently related to armaments will need to be transferred to life-enhancing commodities so that resources are used and incomes generated in life-enhancing ways. All military personnel will need to be demobilised and integrated into civilian life and employment.

Nuclear disarmament for all nuclear weapons states is a matter of great urgency and could be stimulated by unconditional action on the part of any state; perhaps most easily by those like the UK whose weapons are not really independent or necessary, even within the madness of current strategy. Real initiatives in nuclear disarmament by currently nuclear-armed states would give them some moral ground to stand on as they call on others to follow suit, precipitating the reversal of the proliferation process and the progressive dismantling of nuclear capabilities.

There is plenty of potential for alternative employment for military personnel, given the massive financial resources that will be become available. At last sufficient resources – human, technical and financial – will be available for civilian crisis intervention; to help to prevent and diffuse outbreaks of violence (which will be increasingly starved of arms); to come to the rescue of those struck by the disasters resulting from disease, flood, famine and earthquake; and to receive and accommodate all those who have fled from any of the above.

Barack Obama's decision to send military engineers to West Africa to build clinics and isolation wards there, to help deal with the Ebola epidemic, suggests another form of emergency intervention. His belated yet heartening initiative encouraged other governments to follow suit and gave an insight into future possibilities for converting military forces into truly humanitarian ones. The courage of nurses and doctors who have volunteered to work with Ebola patients in the affected countries offers a model of heroism that is potentially sacrificial as any military one and inspiring in its compassion and solidarity.

In the long term, most crucially, perhaps, the technical resources released from the arms industry could make a vital difference to the development and production of green energy sources. (This is an idea already being promoted by the Campaign Against Arms Trade in its 'Arms to Renewables' campaign.[13])

Expertise will need to be applied in the demilitarisation of relationships, drawing on the existing experience and theory of diplomats, nongovernmental peacebuilders and community activists. Adequate resources must be made available for both international diplomacy and the work of local peacemakers. Sufficient international support will need to be given to countries that need to be rebuilt after violent conflict, so that people can begin to feel the benefits of peace.

Education (for all ages) will play an essential role in replacing militarised thinking, enabling people of all ages to develop creative approaches to human relationships and politics, and to develop the skills to address conflict constructively and contribute to positive change. Research and dialogue on the nonviolent exercise of force in cases of emergency would, I believe, yield important new understanding, both practical and philosophical.

As we look to the future we will also need to deal with the global past. Great harm has been done, in action and reaction, and active processes of healing are needed. Part of that healing will be a healing of ideas, as well as hearts, and will stem from an understanding that it is not just 'the other' who holds extreme beliefs. All militarist thinking justifies deliberate, organised and systematic violence and it has made its home in many belief systems.

At different points in history, intercommunal conflict based on belief as a form of identity has taken global proportions. It did in the old wars between Christendom and Islam, between Catholicism and Protestantism, and between radical forms of communism and capitalism. Differences can be lived with, but ideologies, whether secular or religious, that devalue human life and encourage hatred are poisonous and need to be transformed.

They certainly cannot be killed. The dynamic of hatred must be transformed. In the case of the 'war on terror' and violent jihad, urgent action is currently needed, from the international level to

---

13 At the time of writing, a campaign leaflet is available for download at https://www.caat. org.uk/issues/jobs-economy/resources/trade-union-infosheet.pdf [accessed 4 January 2015].

local communities, to find, build or rebuild bridges and begin such a reversal.

Although human beings share their genetic inheritance, there are many different cultural perspectives on life. All have their strengths and weaknesses. Let us learn from each other's strengths. When I think of the grace of some customs and attitudes in Africa, for instance – specifically the emphasis on generosity of spirit and the capacity to forgive – it gives me hope that we can learn much that can help free us from the past.

This is a vast but necessary agenda that I have created in my mind. Others will have additional ideas and different ones. The conversation about them will be part of our engagement in transformation and the ideas will take generations to implement. That is why it is so important that we begin now and say a resounding 'yes' to such an agenda for peace and the 'no' to violence that is needed if we are to move forward in faith and allow our energies to flow in the direction of life.

It is encouraging to think that even in the world of realpolitik, where all too often genuine diplomacy is tried only after sabre-rattling has failed to produce the desired effect, constructive engagement can produce remarkably positive and rapid change in formerly hostile relationships, as witness the impact of the friendship between Margaret Thatcher and Mikhail Gorbachev, the improvement in relationships between the USA and China after Richard Nixon's meeting with Mao Zedong and Zhou Enlai in 1972, and the relaxation of tension between Iran and the West since the end of 2013, when President Hassan Rouhani for the first time openly announced his wish to rebuild and improve relations with Europe and North America.

In all those cases deep social and political problems remain; yet we can take courage from the fact that personal connecting can open up new possibilities. All forms of lasting change necessarily involve the participation of the many in creating new ways of seeing the world and new norms for social living. Right now we need a shift in ideas that will begin a process that is global in its reach and grows from a transformed understanding of power. What a task! Yet once change has begun it can rapidly gather speed.

A Quaker agenda for action

In sum, nonviolence is an absolutely integral part of Quaker life, and our highly ambitious and utterly necessary goal, as members of the worldwide Society of Friends and as global citizens, must be to see acceptance of war transformed into commitment and action to end it; to see the skills of nonviolent assertiveness, conciliation and peacebuilding developed and applied in local, national and international politics; to see 'foreign policy' turned into policy for constructive international relations and solidarity, and the world rapidly demilitarised.

Rabindranath Tagore wrote that 'faith is the bird that feels the light and sings when the dawn is still dark'. Given the hold of old patterns of thinking and the weight of prevalent assumptions, perhaps the most important step that Friends and others can take is to start singing a different song: to express to each other, and share with others, adventurous ideas about the way things could be done, generating circles of conversation about those ideas and beginning to find ways of testing them.

One remarkable step that has already been taken by the American Friends Service Committee (AFSC) and Friends Committee on National Legislation, in consultation with a wider Quaker reference group, is to start translating the vision or agenda that they have into a set of policy proposals. In April 2013, after an extensive consultative process, they published a working paper entitled *Shared Security: Reimagining US Foreign Policy*. It starts from the assumption that preventing war is possible and presents a new vision of security, arguing that old policies are not working and that new ones – like engagement with China – hold much greater promise. It suggests that for instance US militarised foreign policy in Somalia could be replaced by far more encouraging work to engage Somali youth in the quest for peace. It argues that resource cooperation can work far better than resource wars and that nonviolence offers the only way forward in Israel–Palestine.

The approach taken in this US Quaker publication – to couple challenge to existing policies with examples and ideas that offer genuine alternatives – is a constructive and effective way to push forward our own thinking and make the case for the transformation we want to see. Just as it is very hard to move out of a home without having found another one, it is hard to give up old ideas without having new ones to replace them. In fact, change in ideas comes mostly through a process of gradual displacement, and those with experience of genuine peacebuilding can assist in that process (Francis, 2010).

Since that US Quaker document was published, a group of colleagues in Britain (including several Friends) with experience of conflict transformation and peacebuilding met in January 2014 to reflect on the insights they had gained in their work and to translate them into ideas and action for new policy in the UK and internationally. After their second meeting they decided to write a paper for publication that would be used to generate conversation, in all the circles they could reach, about alternatives to the current approach to national security, outlining their concerns about the existing model and offering a different vision for the future. 'Security for the Future: In Search of a New Vision' (also known as the Ammerdown Invitation) was posted online in September 2014, and initial responses have been encouraging.[14]

Meanwhile, programmes within the central work of Quakers in Britain are contributing in important ways to this agenda for change. The current list of programmes and projects undertaken by Quaker Peace & Social Witness (QPSW) within the central work of Britain Yearly Meeting is impressive.[15] It shows at a glance that our yearly meeting is working within all four fields of social and economic justice, human rights, ecosystem protection and peace, locally and globally.

This work upholds our witness to the preciousness of every person, whatever their past and in whatever situation they may find themselves, including those on the margins of society and in need of human solidarity and those entangled in violence and needing to find a way out. In this variety of ways it is helping to develop the conditions for 'positive peace'. The Sustainability programme

---

14 See www.opendemocracy.net/ammerdown-invitation [accessed 4 January 2015].
15 For more information about the work of QPSW see www.quaker.org.uk/qpsw.

of QPSW, which came into being in 2010, not only works for the protection of our planet but seeks to relate the different aspects of our witness to each other.

There are many QPSW programmes within the specific field of peacemaking, along with those of the Quaker United Nations Office and the Quaker Centre for European Affairs. Through these, Friends are lobbying and campaigning for disarmament, helping to broker steps towards arms limitation and demilitarisation, preparing citizens and communities for nonviolent action within their own context, supporting sensitive peace processes in regions affected by political violence, and providing excellent materials for peace education in the UK (where the military are all too active in schools and universities).

I am deeply grateful for the work that is currently done in our name, and for the dedication and imagination of the staff who carry it forward. I sincerely hope that we will continue to support it.

I hope that as we continue to campaign for specific measures of disarmament and demilitarisation, we will set those goals in the context of a wider drive for a profound change in attitudes that will delegitimise war as an institution. I believe that such a movement is on the rise and I trust that Quakers will be contributing in every way possible. After all, we have had a head start with our insights on the things that make for peace (based of course on the insights of someone born more than 1650 years earlier than his disciples, George Fox and his friends). I am heartened to know that so many young Friends in Britain are carrying forward the challenge of our testimony.

We have much to contribute to thinking about global policy change. I hope that we will find a way to identify and pool the experience-based knowledge that we have generated over the years, in the many ways in which we have worked for peace. Already, for instance, I believe that we can play a crucial role in helping to conceptualise and articulate the interdependence between different aspects of sustainable and peaceful coexistence, and this thinking could feed into policy formulations along the lines of those developed by US Friends.

In relation to the development of nonviolent forms of power that can displace war and other political violence, I think that we have the experience and the thinkers to draw out some of the lessons of the 'Arab Spring' and undertake new and substantial thinking about the necessary interplay between nonviolent assertiveness and conciliation. If nonviolent responses to oppressive systems are to be fit for the purpose of delivering peace for all sectors of society, they will need to address the fact that different people have differing and sometimes clashing world views and interests, and that wholesale change that is brought about suddenly, by coercion, even without gunfire, is unlikely to achieve a peace in which all feel that they can participate with dignity and safety.

I understand why people who want radical change often use the language of revolution (I have done it for years myself), but I have come to believe that revolutions, when they are not crushed or blocked and reversed immediately, unless a particularly oppressive and unsupported government is the only obstacle to a unified and peaceful future, are liable to dislocate things in damaging as well as desirable ways and often create new versions of oppression and exclusion. 'Transformation' describes a process in which society is understood as something complex that once torn apart may take several lifetimes to mend, and that it therefore needs to be changed with great care and respect.

A process of deep reflection and hard thinking is needed to address the dilemmas inherent in holding together urgency, right process and long-term goals. We will need to harness both careful analysis and creativity, and let our thinking be informed by the insights of many others. But, like the whole question of militarism, this is a matter of means and ends. What does our faith tell us about how good ends can be achieved? In any situation we need to be asking the question, 'What does love require?'

Nonviolence can require a standing firm (for instance in refusing to participate in violent systems or showing love when it is forbidden); but it always means behaving towards 'the other' in ways that are respectful and do not demonise or repel. Its goal must be to open up common ground, a meeting place where persuading and changing can happen. It is respectful listening and creative, imaginative dialogue that will give the best chance of lasting peace, and the process may take a long time and considerable sacrifice. Nonviolent action informed by this kind of thinking is home territory for Friends. Through the Turning the Tide programme and Quaker conciliation work, Friends have long experience of working in support of citizens' nonviolent action, at home and abroad.

There are other important areas in which Friends can contribute from their experiences and connections and the learning that these have brought. QPSW's work in coordinating the Ecumenical Accompaniment Programme in Palestine and Israel (EAPPI),[16] along with the participation of individual Friends as volunteers in the region, has provided much food for thought on what enables dialogue to be fruitful in such tense and polarised situations and what messages can make a difference.

Dialogue with members of the Jewish community in the UK has also brought valuable insights. It is hard to overstate the importance of the learning that we can draw from this difficult area of our work.

Interfaith dialogue in which Friends have been involved, taking place at the St Ethelburga's Centre for Reconciliation and Peace,[17] which has included a conference involving Jewish and Muslim communities, has been focused on the constant endeavour to re-establish broken connections when both communities feel betrayed. I hope that we can develop our dialogue work to contribute to peacebuilding between different communities and faiths in the UK, which can add to understanding of what is needed in the world at large.

It is vital, whether in particular instances like this one or in the wider arena of deep policy change, that we avoid regarding as enemies those whose policies or actions we oppose. It is with just such people that we need to build bridges of understanding, and in any group or institution there will be people who have some openness to other thinking.

At the global level, the work of the World Council of Churches for 'justice, peace and the integrity of creation' deserves our support and cooperation. If we avoid getting hung up on doctrinal differences

16 See www.eappi.org/.
17 See https://www.stethelburgas.org/.

and focus on the beliefs, insights and commitments that we share, we will find synergy and solidarity in matters very much in line with our own testimony.

The dialogue work of the Quaker United Nations Office brings people together to make personal connections in order to hold fruitful discussions about serious policy issues, for instance in relation to arms limitation or disarmament. Although those involved in the dialogue carry the responsibility of representing their governments, the quality of their interactions – their ability to respect and listen to each other, and to speak both plainly and sincerely – can make a crucial difference to the outcomes of their meetings. Making an effort to create social bonds can also enhance dialogue's effectiveness.

Another Quaker project that has already had a strong impact has been a process undertaken by QPSW and African peacemakers together in order to make known the experiences and inspiration of Africans who are Quakers or are involved in Quaker peacework in Africa. The heart and soul of their responses to traumatic violence are distilled in a beautiful book and exhibition of words and photographs (Chico, 2014). Entitled *This Light that Pushes Me*, this collection of personal testimonies conveys the depth and power of those responses, teaching profound lessons about what is needed to deal with the past and purify the ground for the building of peace. Such purification is needed as much in global relationships as it is in particular communities and countries. The world has much to learn from Africa.

We hear and see so much of the damage that religion can do that it is good to remember that being a people of faith can in itself create positive connections, particularly with others who are searching for peace in the midst of violence. The Quaker experience in conciliation work between a particular set of militant groups is that worshipping together creates a bond, a bond that is at the heart of the trust between us and them, and that binds the rivals to each other. To sing and pray with them has been a moving experience for all concerned.

In his Swarthmore Lecture in 2014 Ben Pink Dandelion emphasised the importance of recognising the different gifts that individual Friends bring to our Society and its work. I would suggest that Friends also have collective gifts to bring to the wider field of peacemaking, while also acknowledging that those gifts may not be ours alone. 'Process' is a key word for Friends. We believe that the way we do things cannot be separated from 'outcomes', since any moment or step leads to another and in each we are called to witness to the same principle and spirit of love. We also bring the power of silence to what we do: a power that can not only restore calm but can sometimes transform processes, creating a safe world of stillness in which souls that have been separated can meet.

Grounds for hope

We have reached a fork in the road and must choose, urgently. If we can find no alternative path to follow, the future for our world is bleak. The culture, machinery and practice of war is the most directly and symbolically destructive manifestation of the violence, disrespect and neglect that disfigure human society and threaten life on earth. It represents a model of power that is as deadly as it is unloving. For us as a Society to accept or tolerate it would be a contradiction of such profundity that it would seem to make nonsense of our faith.

To return to the words of Martin Luther King,

returning violence for violence multiplies violence, adding deeper darkness to a night already devoid of stars. Darkness cannot drive out darkness: only light can do that. Hate cannot drive out hate: only love can do that.

The light and the love at the heart of our faith are needed as never before. If we lose faith in them, we have nothing to offer, to ourselves or to anyone else. Without belief that change is possible, nothing will change; but faith can move mountains. It provides the basis for will, and the will to transform human behaviour has become an existential necessity on a planet in crisis. Humanity's salvation will come, if it does, from a rediscovery of kindness – the caring that comes from a sense of kinship. If there is to be a future for life on our planet that in any way resembles the best of the one we know

now, that sense of kinship needs to be extended to the unbroken chain of life and belonging. If human beings cannot recognise and cherish even each other, what hope is there?

Friends, like many other people of faith, see integrity in terms of translating their professed beliefs into action in a world that does not yet share them. Faith, truth and witness are part of each other, and our 'peace testimony' lies at the core of our one testimony to the life and power of love. It is not something to be left to 'Friends House'. It calls for our whole-hearted support and needs to be at home in the hearts of all Friends. If we are, as Ben suggests, a 'community rooted in the experience of transformation', (Dandelion, 2104, p. 9) we must draw on that experience to give us the faith and courage to act for world transformation.

We cannot look two ways. To say 'yes' to peace we must say a final 'no' to war and join together, heart and soul, in the task of creating peace by peaceful means, speaking with one authentic and passionate voice. Our faith is needed in the world, and urgently. If we exercise it, it will grow in us.

While our Britain Yearly Meeting programmes continue in our name, with our support, the efforts of special-interest groups will continue to augment them, along with Friends' local work for peace – whether it is undertaken within Quaker initiatives or together with the many others who are moving in the same direction. Some of us are already at full stretch, working on our bit of the patchwork of positive peace: projects and campaigns for ecological protection, lifestyle change (which must involve us all), human rights for refugees, neighbourhood mediation, restorative justice, fair trade, peace in the Middle East, running local food banks – the list could be very long.

Other Friends focus their main efforts on public resistance to war and yet others combine campaigning with practical work to end violence in specific conflicts, at home or abroad. My hope is that they will use that experience in broader work to demilitarise minds, societies and international relationships, using the wealth of their collective experience to inform both public debate and off-the-record conversations. What matters about these different forms of witness is that we understand that they are all part of one testimony to life and love.

The world is experiencing a great darkness. If we truly have a light to guide us, now is not the time to hide it, to let it waver or, worst of all, to let it go out. This is a testing time, when our faithfulness is needed as never before: a time for us to support each other in holding our light aloft. Our numbers matter little in comparison to this. If we attend to this, they may or may not grow, but at least we will not have failed to put our faith into practice.

Some of us may not be in a position to work in any concerted way for peace, but we can still be witnesses. We all have opportunities to listen to, question and speak to others, whether in conversation with our neighbours, with the person next to us in the bus queue, or on the street when we see something that calls for comment or challenge. Exercising the 'civil courage' to speak out is a responsibility and power that we all share. For some of us it may mean undertaking that media interview or speaking engagement that we might have preferred to refuse. Many of us could make the extra effort to write to the paper, visit our MP or take part in a vigil. And, vitally, those who can do none of these things can uphold those of us who can and do. We badly need that loving support.

None of us can be experts on everything, but we can make it our business to have given some thought to the different issues that we learn of through others or meet through our reading, listening and viewing. We can relate them to our faith and reflect on them, alone and with others, in meeting for worship, with invited speakers and in group discussion, building a picture or mind map of the ways in which different aspects and mechanisms of human relationships and behaviour relate to each other, and where the spirit of love can bring about change. We can always speak out on our principles or values, even when we cannot apply them in detail to the matter in hand.

Sometimes we may feel that it is all so complex and that so much is wrong that the transformation we long for is impossible: the vision of peace for people and planet is in fact a mirage. I confess that I do not believe in any perfect society, any more than I believe in a perfect self. For me, any idea of wholeness needs to embrace imperfection. I do believe, however, that if we, with others, can generate the will, in ever widening circles, we can build the norms, frameworks, systems and relationships that can bring out the best in people, rather than tolerating or encouraging the worst. I do believe that by steadfastly building the values and practices of cooperation and empathy, and unmasking and rejecting the kinds of violence that are currently accepted, we can make them rare and shocking, rather than all too familiar.

Although much violence still takes place unseen in this country, its visible manifestations in day-to-day life are already largely unacceptable. It would seem that gross inequalities between different kinds of people within a society, which can be classified as structural violence, cause major and manifold problems in any society (see Wilkinson and Pickett, 2010) and make for greater levels of overt violence. Peaceable behaviour and social responsibility can be expected to grow with greater social and economic justice, globally as well as nationally. Closing the gap, sharing resources and simplifying the greedy and environmentally damaging lifestyles of the 'developed' world will be as vital to peace as peace is to them. The good news is that progress on one front will accelerate progress on another.

Although all sorts of violence persist, here in the UK and in a good many other societies, general social acceptance of direct personal violence has decreased in my lifetime. Our task is to make the connection between personal violence and the organised, nationally sanctioned violence of war.

Human beings are highly intelligent and creative. They are also, when spiritually and emotionally grounded, capable of deep wisdom. Even the technological capacities that we have so greatly perverted can be used for great good. Our powers of communication, always strong, are now amplified in ways that make global reach possible; a movement of movements is already under way.

The tide is potentially on the turn, with tow and counter-tow. The power model at the top of the still prevailing hierarchical system seems to remain unchanged, but a very different sort of power is growing from below. Its energy needs to be harnessed and directed, and we must be part of it. There are others heading in the same direction whose persistence is motivated simply by compassion and moral conviction. They need our solidarity and, having our own history and inspiration, we have particular insights to bring: insights that are constantly refreshed and developed by engagement.

We cannot be and do everything, either as individuals or collectively. Nor can we know how the needed transformation will take shape. We must analyse and reanalyse the things we want to change, devise and re-devise strategic plans. At the same time we will do well to keep in mind the advice of the great Spanish poet Antonio Machado (2003): 'Walker, there is no road, the road is made by walking.'

Putting one step in front of another, we can rely on what we call 'the leadings of the spirit', which others might call intuition. Whatever words we use, we must engage heart, mind and soul in the work to which we are called. Good, sharp thinking is needed, along with creative imagination and keen intuition – the antennae that help us to sense the energy and opportunities of the moment. We also need the wisdom that goes deeper and sees further.

We have each other to check, challenge and enrich our thinking, which is a vital strength. Quaker processes of collective discernment can make movement laborious and slow, but our reliance on the guidance that comes from the spirit within and beyond us all is essential if we are to step sure-footedly into the dark, in faith. Our ways of working together need to be as straightforward, flexible and joined up as possible, to allow cooperation and energy to flow and to balance accountability with trust. We have dedicated staff and officers in Britain Yearly Meeting who will help us to achieve that grounded effectiveness. It is the spirit that will lift us.

Of one thing I am certain: that laughter is essential to our spiritual energy. The road ahead may be daunting and at times sad and frustrating, yet there can and must be joy in the mix or we will never stay the course. To save life we must love and celebrate it too.

APPENDIX

Stages and processes in conflict transformation

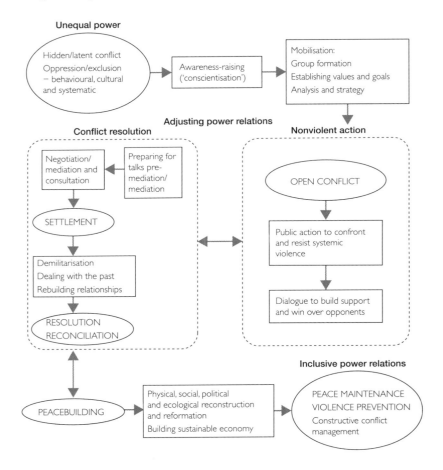

BIBLIOGRAPHY

A strong Britain in an age of uncertainty: The national security strategy (2010). UK Government White Paper. London: HMSO. Available online at https://www.gov.uk/government/uploads/system/uploads/attachment_data/file/61936/national-security-strategy.pdf [accessed 30 December 2014].

American Friends Service Committee and Friends Committee on National Legislation (2013) *Shared security: Reimagining US foreign policy*. A Working Paper. Philadelphia and Washington: American Friends Service Committee and Friends Committee on National Legislation. Available for download at http://sharedsecurity.files.wordpress.com/2013/05/shared-security_v8-for-distribution.pdf [accessed 4 January 2015].

Baum, Dan (2004). 'The price of valor' in *The New Yorker*, 12 July, 44–52. Available online at http://www.newyorker.com/magazine/2004/07/12/the-price-of-valor [accessed 29 December 2014].

Berdal, Mats and David Malone, eds. (2000). *Greed and grievance: Economic agendas in civil wars*. Colorado and London: Lynne Rienner.

Chenoweth, Erica and Maria J. Stephan (2011). *Why civil resistance works: The strategic logic of nonviolent conflict*. New York, NY: Columbia University Press.

Chico, Laura Shipler (2010). 'Turning the tide in Kenya' in *Quaker News* 77, 8–9. Available online at http://www.quaker.org.uk/quaker-news-77-winter-2010-turning-tide-kenya [accessed 29 December 2014].

Chico, Laura Shipler, ed. (2014). *This light that pushes me*. London: Quaker Books.

Clark, Howard (2000). *Civil resistance in Kosovo*. London: Pluto Press.

Curle, Adam (1981). *True justice: Quaker peace makers and peace making*. The 1981 Swarthmore Lecture. London: Quaker Home Service.

Dandelion, Ben Pink (2014). *Open for transformation: Being Quaker*. The 2014 Swarthmore Lecture. London: Quaker Books.

Dao, James (2013). 'Drone pilots are found to get stress disorders much as those in combat do' in *The New York Times*, 23 February, A9. Available online at http://www.nytimes.com/2013/02/23/us/drone-pilots-found-to-get-stress-disorders-much-as-those-in-combat-do.html?_r=0 [accessed 30 December 2014].

Dawkins, Richard (1976). *The selfish gene*. Oxford: Oxford University Press.

Eisler, Riane (1990). *The chalice and the blade: Our history, our future*. London: Unwin Paperbacks.

Ferguson, Brian (2003). 'The birth of war' in *Natural History*, July/August 2003.

Francis, Diana (2001). *Lessons from Kosovo/a: Alternatives to war*. London: Quaker Peace & Social Witness.

Francis, Diana (2002). *People, peace and power: Transformation in action*. London: Pluto Press.

Francis, Diana (2004). *Rethinking war and peace*. London: Pluto Press.

Francis, Diana (2010). *From pacification to peacebuilding: A call to global transformation*. London: Pluto Press.

Freire, Paulo (1972). *Pedagogy of the oppressed*. London: Penguin.

Galtung, Johan (1964). 'Editorial' in *Journal of Peace Research*, 1 (1), 1–4.

Galtung, Johan (1990). 'Cultural violence' in *Journal of Peace Research*, 27 (3), 291–305.

Galtung, Johan (2005). 'Violence, peace and peace research' in Matthew Evangelista, ed., *Peace studies: Critical concepts*. London: Routledge

Glover, Jonathan (2001). *Humanity: A moral history of the twentieth century*. London: Pimlico.

Harris, Geoff, ed. (2004). *Achieving security in sub-Saharan Africa: Cost effective alternatives to the military*. Pretoria: Institute for Security Studies.

Incentives, sanctions and conditionality in peacemaking (2008). London: Conciliation Resources. Accord policy brief. Available online at http://www.c-r.org/sites/default/files/Accord%2019_Powersofpersuasion_policybrief_2008_ENG.pdf [accessed

30 December 2014].

Kelly, Raymond (2000). *Warless societies and the origin of war.* Michigan: University of Michigan Press.

Lunn, Pam (2011). *Costing not less than everything: Sustainability and spirituality in challenging times.* The 2011 Swarthmore Lecture. London, Quaker Books.

Machado, Antonio (2003). 'Proverbs and Songs no. 29' in *Border of a dream: Selected poems.* Translated by Willis Barnstone. Port Townsend, Washington: Copper Canyon Press.

Martin, Brian (1984). *Uprooting war,* chapter 3: 'Social defence'. London: Freedom Press. An updated (1990) edition is available online at http://www.bmartin.cc/pubs/90uw/ [accessed 5 January 2015].

Martin, Brian (1993). *Social defence, social change.* London: Freedom Press.

Martin, Brian (2004). 'Defending without the military' in Geoff Harris, ed. *Achieving security in sub-Saharan Africa: Cost effective alternatives to the military.* Pretoria: Institute for Security Studies, pp. 43–55.

Morris, Desmond (1967). *The naked ape: A zoologist's study of the human animal.* London: Jonathan Cape.

Philips, Adam and Taylor, Barbara (2009). *On kindness.* London: Macmillan.

Quaker faith & practice: The book of Christian discipline of the Yearly Meeting of the Religious Society of Friends (Quakers) in Britain (2013). Fifth edition. London: Religious Society of Friends (Quakers) in Britain.

Rogers, Paul (2012). *Chances for peace in the second decade – What is going wrong and what we must do.* Oxford Research Group Special Briefing. London: Oxford Research Group. Published online at http://www.oxfordresearchgroup.org.uk/publications/paul_rogers_monthly_global_security_briefings/org_special_briefing_chances_peace_second, where it is available as a pdf download [accessed 4 January 2015].

Sharp, Gene; with the assistance of Bruce Jenkins (1990). *Civilian-based defense: A post-military weapons system.* Princeton, NJ: Princeton University Press.

Solzhenitsyn, Alexandr I. (1974). *The Gulag Archipelago 1918–1956: An Experiment in Literary Investigation.* London: Collins/Fontana.

Waal, Frans de (1997). *Good natured: The origins of right and wrong in humans and other animals.* Cambridge, Mass.: Harvard University Press.

Wilkinson, Richard and Kate Pickett (2010). *The spirit level: Why equality is better for everyone.* London: Penguin Books.

Wink, Walter (1983). *Jesus and nonviolence: A third way.* London: Facet Publishing.